KU-491-484

vrindavana-chandra
krishna

Pastimes of Krishna in Vrindavana

Based on
KRISHNA - The Supreme Personality of Godhead

by
His Divine Grace
A.C. Bhaktivedanta Swami Prabhupada
Founder-Acharya of ISKCON

Adapted for children by
Yaduraja Dasa

International Society for Krishna Consciousness
Hare Krishna Hill, Chord Road, Bangalore-10

A book in English
Vrindava-Chandra Krishna
Pastimes of Krishna in Vrindavana

Based on :
Krishna - The Supreme Personality of Godhead

by His Divine Grace
A.C. Bhaktivedanta Swami Prabhupada
Founder - Acharya of ISKCON

Adapted for childred by
Yaduraja Dasa

Published by The Sankirtana Seva Trust, Bangalore
Printed at **Brilliant Printers Pvt. Ltd.**, Bangalore
[Total Pages : 232 + 16 - 1/8 Crown Size]

© 2005, All Right Reserved

Price : Rs. 45/-   **ISBN** : 81-8239-006-0

First Printing : 2004 : 5,000 copies
Second Printing : 2005 : 10,000 copies

Adress for correspondence :
Secretary
ISKCON
Hare Krishna Hill, Chord Road,
Rajajinagar, Bangalore - 560 010.
Ph : 080-23471956
E-mail : infodesk@iskconbangalore.org
www.iskconbangalore.org

Contents

Introduction

In the ancient Vedic literatures it is said that the cause and origin of everything is Lord Sri Krishna. The name Krishna means 'all-attractive'. If someone is exceptionally rich, famous, renounced, clever, strong, or beautiful then we find such a person to some extent attractive. Just imagine someone who is the wealthiest, the most beautiful, famous, renounced, intelligent person in the whole universe. That person, who has all those attractive qualities to an unlimited degree, is called Krishna. He is so attractive that anyone who sincerely tries to know Him will immediately become attracted. Krishna is God and is referred to by many names, according to different languages and cultures, such as Allah, Jehovah, Christos and Govinda. In the *Bhagavad-gita* it is stated that anyone who hears and properly understands the pastimes of Lord Krishna will be able to leave this material world, which is full of suffering, and return to His eternal abode. This book gives an account of Krishna's wonderful activities when He last appeared on Earth, in His original form, five thousand years ago. It has been adapted for children from the book 'Krishna—The Supreme Personality of Godhead', authored by His Divine Grace, A.C. Bhaktivedanta Swami Prabhupada.

* * *

Prologue:
The Tears of Mother Earth

Five thousand years ago the world was overburdened by the vast armies of many demons who were posing themselves as kings. At that time the whole world became disturbed and Mother Earth, or Bhumi as she is also called, took the form of a cow and with tears in her eyes approached Lord Brahma, the first created being in this universe. After hearing Bhumi describe the terrible position of the Earth, Lord Brahma became much distressed and at once set out for the ocean of milk, accompanied by Bhumi and all the *devatas*, to seek the help of Lord Vishnu. Lord Vishnu assured Brahma that He would soon personally appear on Earth in His original form as Sri Krishna, in order to destroy all the demons and protect His devotees. He told Lord Brahma and all the *devatas* that before He made His divine appearance as the son of Vasudeva, they should all take birth in pious families on Earth in order to assist Him. Thus the stage was set for a huge battle between the forces of good and evil that would eventually lead to the great battle of Kurukshetra.

* * *

1. The Curse

"I knew you'd like it," chuckled the powerful King Kamsa as he saw his sister Devaki's expression, "I had it built especially for your wedding. Just see how it is encrusted with the most valuable gems, and look at those horses, finest stallions in the world. Come on, climb aboard, and you too Vasudeva; don't keep your new bride waiting."

Devaki smiled appreciatively as she climbed up into the fabulous, golden chariot with her husband, cheered by thousands of admiring onlookers who thronged the decorated streets, throwing flower petals and scented water.

"Kamsa, please let me take the reins," insisted Vasudeva, "the king should never have to drive a chariot."

"But it is tradition; the brother must drive his newly wedded sister to her home. I insist Vasudeva, it is my great pleasure, so please sit and enjoy the procession." With that Kamsa shook the reins with his powerful arms and whipped the horses into motion. They set off along the main street of Mathura accompanied by thousands of soldiers, elephants and horses, their armour glinting in the bright sunlight. Amongst the jubilant crowd were many musicians playing conch-shells, bugles and kettledrums, all in glorification of the royal occasion. Kamsa laughed as he stood waving to his citizens, while Vasudeva and Devaki sat at the back of the open chariot smiling at the adoring crowd and each other. All at once the sky darkened, and a deep rumbling sound made all the horses rear up in fear. The smile on Kamsa's face vanished as he looked up at a strange glow in the heavens. Then a booming voice filled the air:

"Kamsa, you are such a fool! You do not know that the eighth child of your sister will kill you."

On hearing the prophecy from the sky, Kamsa immediately caught hold of Devaki's hair, his large black moustache twitching with rage.

"What is this, your child will kill me? Come here Devaki." Kamsa drew his sword to slit his sister's throat. The crowd gasped as Vasudeva leapt forward to hold his arm.

"My dear brother-in-law, do not kill your own sister." Vasudeva pleaded, "Kamsa, you are the most famous king of the Bhoja dynasty; how can you kill a woman at this auspicious time of her marriage? Why should you be so afraid of death? Death is already born along with your birth. Please put down your sword, I beg of you."

"Your child… will kill me?" Kamsa rasped in disbelief.

"Kamsa, this situation is so delicate, don't you see," Vasudeva shouted, as he struggled to hold back Kamsa's razor sharp blade, "if you kill her, it will ruin your reputation. What will people say of the king who murdered his own sister on the day of her marriage?"

Kamsa took no notice; he was intent on ending his sister's life then and there.

"Listen to me, please," yelled Vasudeva, "you are in no danger now since we have no children. I promise that if we have any sons I shall present all of them to you to do with as you wish."

His chest heaving with anger, Kamsa slowly lowered his sword.

"You would do that; bring me any children born to Devaki?"

"Yes, I give you my solemn oath," Vasudeva replied.

Kamsa knew the value of Vasudeva's word of honour, and so was convinced by his argument. He decided that, for the time being at least, his sister's life would be spared.

"Good. Very well, then let the royal procession continue." At this command, Kamsa yanked the reins and the carriage lurched forward. But the young couple at the back were no longer smiling and waving; they sat in solemn silence.

When Devaki gave birth to their first son, Vasudeva kept his promise and promptly brought the baby before Kamsa.

"I am so pleased you have kept your word," said Kamsa as Vasudeva stood before him cradling the infant. Vasudeva held the child out for Kamsa to take. Kamsa looked at the child, then up at the sad face of its father. His eyes softened.

"My dear Vasudeva, I am not in any danger from this child. It is your eighth son who is destined to kill. You can take him back."

With tears of relief, Vasudeva returned home to Devaki, though in his heart he knew he could not trust Kamsa.

* * *

2. A Visit from Narada Muni

"Your majesty, the great sage Narada Muni requests an audience with you."

Kamsa stood from his throne at this news from one of his servants.

"Show him in immediately; offer him all respects," said Kamsa urgently.

As the great doors opened, the palace filled with the enchanting sound of Narada Muni's voice as he sang the name of Narayana accompanied by his melodious *vina*. He seemed to float through the air as he entered Kamsa's chambers.

"It is a great honour that you have come, please be seated." Kamsa gestured to a large throne near to his, "So, what has brought you here?"

"Kamsa, I have grave news for you," said Narada Muni, as he placed his *vina* down gently by his side, "I hear that you have spared the life of Devaki's first born child."

"That is correct; he was of no threat to me," Kamsa replied, generously.

"Kamsa, do you realize that many *devatas* have descended from their heavenly abodes to take birth here on Earth just to assist Lord Krishna in your destruction?"

"Have they?" Kamsa said, surprised.

"Therefore any one of Devaki's children could be your mortal enemy, not just the eighth," warned Narada Muni.

"What...?"

"Did you know that in your previous birth you were a demon named Kalanemi, and that you met your death at the hands of Lord Vishnu?"

Kamsa was now extremely concerned since he knew that Vishnu was none other than Lord Krishna.

"You took birth in the Bhoja dynasty, and by your activities have made the Yadu dynasty your enemy. It is in the Yadu dynasty that Lord Krishna, the cause of all causes, the origin of all incarnations, will make His divine appearance. That is why I felt I should warn you, oh great one."

"But why are you helping me? Your advice has convinced me of only one thing, that all Devaki's children must be killed. Why would you, a saintly *brahmana*, want that?"

"The more atrocities you perform," answered the sage, "the faster my Lord will appear here in this world to destroy all miscreants such as yourself. Now I bid your leave."

Saying that, Narada Muni left, once more chanting the name of Narayana. Kamsa sat, stony faced, thinking to himself: "So, the *devatas* think they can get the better of me do they? I'll see about that." He then called for his Chief Minister.

"I want my father, Ugrasena, thrown in prison within the hour."

"The emperor!" asked the minister in disbelief.

"His armies are loyal to me; they will obey my order. I need him put away so I can also imprison Vasudeva and Devaki," answered Kamsa.

"Yes my lord, I understand," said the minister.

"I cannot afford to be lenient any longer," said Kamsa, clenching the handle of his sword.

* * *

3. The Divine Plan Unfolds

Very soon Kamsa had imprisoned his father, sister and brother-in-law. King Kamsa also made alliances with every other demoniac king on the face of the Earth. After making many such allies, he boldly declared himself the supreme ruler of the world, and began to attack the Yadu dynasty, into which Krishna and His devotees were meant to take birth. In this way he did everything within his power to secure his own safety.

Within the fortress prison, shackled in heavy, iron chains, Vasudeva and Devaki gave birth to six male children year after year, and Kamsa, thinking each to be his enemy, killed them all one after another. Then, by Krishna's arrangement, His expansion known as Balarama appeared within Devaki's womb. Devaki was overwhelmed with both joy and sadness. She was blissful since she knew that Lord Vishnu had taken shelter within her womb, but at the same time she was sorry because as soon as her child was born, Kamsa would kill Him. At that time the Supreme Personality of Godhead, Krishna, ordered the appearance of Yogamaya, His internal potency, and He instructed her thus:

"I want you to transfer the child in Devaki's womb to the womb of Rohini, one of the wives of Vasudeva, after which I shall personally appear in the womb of Devaki with My full potencies. I also want you to appear as the daughter of Nanda and Yashoda in Vrindavana." Krishna instructed.

After Yogamaya took Balarama from the womb of Devaki, Kamsa thought her seventh pregnancy had been a miscarriage. Krishna then mystically entered the mind of Vasudeva and was then transferred to the heart of Devaki. When Krishna entered the heart of Devaki she became very beautiful and effulgent.

"Are you sure she is pregnant your majesty?" Asked Kamsa's Chief Minister.

"Of course I'm sure, have you not seen her? She practically glows! She has never looked more radiant. This is the eighth child she carries, the one who is destined to kill me. What is to be done with Devaki? Krishna has come to carry out the mission of the *devatas*. And even if I immediately kill Devaki, His mission cannot be stopped."

Kamsa wrung his hands as he spoke.

"I say we kill her now your majesty," the minister advised.

"But if I kill Devaki, Krishna will simply enforce His supreme will even more strongly. To kill Devaki now would be a most abominable act. My reputation would be ruined. Devaki is a woman, she is under my shelter and she is pregnant. If I kill her the results of all my pious activities, along with my duration of life, will be finished."

"You must act in self defense my lord," pleaded the minister.

"A person who is too cruel is as good as dead, even in this lifetime. And after death he is sent down to the darkest regions of hell."

With all these considerations Kamsa finally decided not to kill Devaki right away, but to wait for the child to be born, thinking that he could kill Him just as he had done previously with the others. He began to think of Krishna or Vishnu constantly, day and night. He could not get Krishna out of his mind.

At this time, many *devatas* including Lord Brahma and Lord Shiva, accompanied by great sages like Narada Muni, appeared invisibly in the prison house of Kamsa. They began to pray to the Supreme Personality of Godhead:

"Our dear Lord, people are puzzled that the eternal form of Krishna has two hands, two legs and moves among human beings exactly like one of them. This eternal, divine form of Your Lordship gives ever-increasing transcendental pleasure to the devotees, but for the non-devotees it is most dangerous. Dear Lord, when You appear in Your different incarnations, You take different names and forms according to different situations. Lord Krishna is Your original name and form, and this name indicates Your all-attractive nature."

After worshiping the transcendental form of the Lord, all the *devatas* and sages departed for their heavenly abodes, leaving Vasudeva and Devaki with the ecstasy of the Lord's presence.

* * *

4. The Birth of Lord Krishna

When the time came for the Lord's appearance, the positions of all the planets became particularly favourable. Auspicious stars were visible in the sky, and in all towns, villages and pasturing grounds and within the minds of everyone there were signs of good fortune. In all directions there was an atmosphere of peace and prosperity. The rivers were flowing with crystal clear waters, and the lakes were fragrantly decorated with lotus flowers. The forests were full of beautiful birds which began to sing with sweet voices, while the peacocks danced and sang with their consorts. The wind blew pleasantly, carrying the aroma of different flowers, and the sensation of bodily touch became most pleasing. The demoniac kings had tried to stop all Vedic sacrifices, preventing the *brahmanas* from holding fire ceremonies in their own houses; but now all such difficulties eased. Once more the *brahmanas* found their homes quite pleasant to make offerings and their minds became full of joy when they heard transcendental vibrations in the sky announcing the appearance of the Supreme Personality of Godhead. In the heavenly planets, the angels along with their wives began to dance. The great sages and *devatas*, being pleased, began to shower flowers. The seashore was splashed by gentle waves, and above the sea, clouds began to thunder most pleasingly.

Then, when the Earth was ready, Lord Vishnu appeared

in the darkness of night before Vasudeva and Devaki. They saw His wonderful, effulgent four-armed form, His hands holding a conchshell, club, disc and lotus flower. He was decorated with the mark of *shrivatsa*, wearing the jewelled necklace of the *kaustubha* stone, dressed in yellow silk, appearing dazzling like a bright blackish cloud, wearing a helmet bedecked with the *vaidurya* stone, valuable bracelets, earrings and similar other ornaments all over His body and an abundance of raven black hair on His head. Due to the extraordinary features of the child, Vasudeva was struck with wonder.

"Generally, when a male child is born," he thought, "people observe the occasion with jubilant celebrations, but what can I do imprisoned here like this?"

Since he could not physically do anything, within his mind Vasudeva gave thousands of cows to the *brahmanas*. When Vasudeva was convinced that the newborn child was the Supreme Personality of Godhead Himself, he bowed down with folded hands:

"My dear Lord," Vasudeva began to pray, "I can understand You are the original source of the material energy, just as the sun is the source of the sunshine. I understand that You have appeared in order to kill the uncivilized Kamsa and his followers. But as soon as he hears about it, he will immediately appear with all kinds of weapons to kill You."

After Vasudeva's prayer, Devaki, the mother of Krishna, offered her prayers too:

"My dear Lord, I request You to save me from the cruel hands of the son of Ugrasena, Kamsa. Dear Lord, I am

Vasudeva carries Krishna to Vrindavana

Krishna kills the cart demon

Krishna and Balarama's name-giving ceremony

Krishna shows mother Yashoda
the universe in His mouth

Krishna bound by His mother's love

Krishna confronts the Bakasura demon

The cowherd boys enter Aghasura's open mouth

The cowherd men meet their sons at the foot of
the Govardhana hill

Krishna chastises the Kaliya serpent

Balarama slays the demon Pralambasura

Krishna swallows the forest fire

Krishna lifts the Govardhana hill

Krishna rescues Nanda Maharaja
from the abode of Varuna

The *gopis* imitate Krishna's pastimes

Krishna fights Chanura during the
wrestling match at Mathura

Sandipani Muni instructs Krishna and Balarama

afraid because as soon as Kamsa understands that You have appeared, he might try to harm You. So I request that for the time being You become invisible to our material eyes, and then Kamsa will not be able to hurt you." On hearing the prayers of Devaki, the Lord replied:

"My dear mother, long ago both you and your husband performed severe austerities for twelve thousand years of the *devatas*, desiring some wonderful benediction from Me. I was most pleased with you and at that time I also appeared before you in this form and granted you any wish you might have. At that time you asked for Me to be born as your son and I gave you the benediction that I would do so three times. The first time I was known as Prishnigarbha, born of Prishni and Sutapa, the next birth I was Vamanadeva, born of Aditi and Kashyapa, and now for the third time I am born as Krishna from you. My dear father and mother, you have therefore raised Me many times as your child with great affection and love, and I am therefore very pleased and obliged to you. I assure you that this time you shall go back home, back to Godhead, on account of your perfection in your mission. I know you are concerned about Me and afraid of Kamsa. Therefore I order you to take Me immediately to Gokula and exchange Me with the daughter who has just been born to Yashoda."

The Lord then turned Himself into a beautiful baby boy, and remained silent. At the same time Yogamaya was born to Nanda and Yashoda. By Her mystical influence all the residents of Kamsa's palace, especially the doorkeepers, were overwhelmed with deep sleep, and all the palace doors suddenly opened on their own, even though they were barred and shackled with iron chains. The night was dark, but as soon as Vasudeva stepped outside with Krishna, he could see everything just as in the sunlight. At the same time there was thunder in the sky and severe rainfall.

While Vasudeva was carrying his son Krishna in the falling rain, Lord Sesha (who is actually Balarama) in the shape of a many-headed serpent, spread His hood over the head of Vasudeva like an umbrella so he would not be hampered by the rain. Vasudeva came to the bank of the river Yamuna and saw that its waters were roaring with high waves and foam. Somehow the river opened up and allowed Vasudeva to cross easily, just as the great Indian Ocean gave a path to Lord Rama. On the other side, he headed towards Gokula, where he saw that all the cowherd men were fast asleep. Silently he entered the house of Nanda and Yashoda and exchanged his son with the newly born baby girl. Then he returned to the prison of Kamsa and silently put the girl on the lap of Devaki. He again clamped the shackles on his limbs in order to fool Kamsa's guards.

Mother Yashoda knew she had given birth to a baby, but because she was so tired from the labour, she fell fast asleep. When she awoke, she could not remember whether she had given birth to a boy or a girl.

* * *

5. Goddess Durga

The gatekeepers awoke to the sound of the newborn child crying.

"Your majesty, please wake up," the chief minister shook Kamsa as he lay in his bed, "it has happened my lord, the child is born." Kamsa shot up like a bolt from his bed.

"Then we must go to the prison house," he said, throwing on some robes and strapping on his sword, "now the cruel death of my life is born!"

On seeing her brother approaching through the prison doors, Devaki prayed meekly:

"Oh dear brother, I know you are afraid, but please do not kill this female child."

"Female child?" said Kamsa, confused.

"It is just a little girl," said Devaki, hoping her brother would take pity this time.

"It is a trick my lord, whatever it is, kill it," urged the minister.

"Kamsa, I promise that this child will be the wife of your son; don't kill her."

"Give us the child," demanded Kamsa's jail keeper.

"Kamsa, the prophecy said you are to be killed by a male child, not a girl, so please do not kill her. My dear brother, you have killed so many of my new born children. I do not blame *you* for this," said Devaki, looking at his minister, "you have been advised by demoniac friends."

"Just hand over the child," demanded Kamsa, losing patience. Vasudeva watched in horror, his arms chained helplessly to the wall.

"I beg you to leave me this one child, please! Let her live as my daughter!" pleaded Devaki.

"Give it to me now," yelled Kamsa as he forcibly grabbed the newborn child and attempted to dash her mercilessly on the stone floor.

But the baby slipped out of his hands, flew up into the sky and then appeared with eight arms holding a bow, lance, arrows, sword, conchshell, disc, club and shield. This was Krishna's servant, Yogamaya, in the form of the Goddess Durga and she was decorated with attractive garments, flower garlands and ornaments. Kamsa gasped as he looked up at the amazing personality. From above, the goddess called down to Kamsa:

"Kamsa! You rascal, how could you ever kill me? The child who will destroy you is already safely born and is somewhere in this world. Don't be so cruel to your poor sister."

After hearing these words, Kamsa became overwhelmed with fear. Out of pity, and panic, he quickly released Vasudeva and Devaki from their shackles and spoke to them most politely:

"My dear sister and brother-in-law, I have acted just like a demon in killing my own nephews—your children. I do not know what will be the result of these envious acts. Probably I shall be sent to the hell where the killers of *brahmanas* go. I am surprised, however, that the celestial prophecy has not come true. I see it is not only in human society that false propaganda is found. Now it appears that even the celestial denizens speak lies. I committed so many sins because I believed in the prophecy. I request that you not be sorry for the death of your children, since the soul remains intact eternally. Please excuse the atrocities I have committed against you. I am poor-hearted, and you are so great-hearted, so take compassion upon me and forgive me."

While Kamsa was speaking to his brother-in-law and sister, tears flowed from his eyes, and he fell down at their feet. Believing the words of Durga-devi, Kamsa quickly released them both, personally unlocking their iron chains. When Devaki saw her brother was so repentant, she also became pacified and forgot all his crimes against her children. Vasudeva also, forgetting all past incidents, spoke smilingly to Kamsa:

"My dear fortunate brother-in-law," said Vasudeva, "what you are saying about the material body and the soul is correct. Every living entity is born ignorant, misunderstanding this material body to be his self and in this way forgetting his eternal relationship with the Supreme Personality of Godhead."

At Vasudeva's kind, forgiving words Kamsa's guilt subsided, and with their permission he returned to his palace with a relieved mind.

* * *

6. Kamsa's Change of Heart

The next day Kamsa called all his counsellors together and boastfully narrated to them all the incidents of the previous night.

"So it seems the prophecy was false. As you can all see I am alive and well; forgiven by both my sister and brother-in-law who are now perfectly happy, and living in their home."

However, Kamsa's counsellors did not share his glowing optimism.

"Did not the goddess Durga simply re-confirm the prophecy my lord?" Asked one, awkwardly.

"Is it not also a fact that this Krishna could be anywhere for all we know, just waiting to strike?" asked another.

"Well He did not strike. As you see, I stand here before you safe and sound," but Kamsa's confident mood was starting to slip away. In desperation he turned to his most trusted adviser for his opinion.

"Your majesty, we must now make immediate arrangements to kill all children born within the last ten days in all towns, counties, villages and pasturing grounds. Let us execute this plan with all the force at our disposal." A buzz of approval met the minister's words.

"Kill all the children, what about Goddess Durga and the other *devatas*?" Kamsa spluttered.

"The *devatas* are always afraid of fighting with us my

lord; they will not dare try to stop us. They may shout curses from the sky if they like, but they fear your immeasurable strength. We have nothing to worry about. They are proud of being great fighters in peacetime outside the field of war, but they flee like cowards in the face of a real fight."

"But why take the risk of confronting Vishnu and His supporters?" Kamsa argued as another minister stood to speak:

"If there is some disease in the body which is neglected, it worsens and becomes incurable. Therefore, your majesty, we must now be very careful of the *devatas* in case they *do* become too strong for us to subdue. The *devatas'* strength comes from Lord Vishnu, and His biggest supporters are the *brahmanas*. So, I suggest we begin by killing all the *brahmanas* and the great sages who are in charge of performing Vedic sacrifices. And above all let us kill all the cows, which are the source of butter, so necessary for performing sacrifices to Vishnu. Killing the sages, *brahmanas* and cows is the same as killing Lord Vishnu in my opinion."

"Please give us your permission to kill all these creatures," pleaded yet another minister.

"Very well, yes, these are all good suggestions. I am fortunate to be blessed with such trustworthy and wise counsel. Thank you all. We shall put these plans into immediate effect," said Kamsa, convinced by the arguments of all his demoniac ministers.

* * *

7. The Meeting of Nanda Maharaja and Vasudeva

The next day, in the village of Vrindavana, it was declared that a male child had been born to Yashoda. Many *brahmanas* assembled and began chanting auspicious mantras, accompanied by people singing songs, and playing bugles and kettledrums, while astrologers performed the birth ceremony. Nanda Maharaja distributed 200,000 cows in charity to the *brahmanas,* all gorgeously decorated with cloth and ornaments, along with hills of grain decorated with golden-bordered cloth.

When all the ecstatic cowherd men and women heard that Nanda Maharaja, the father of Krishna, was celebrating the birth ceremony of his son, they became instantly joyful. They dressed themselves with costly garments and ornamented their bodies with different kinds of earrings and necklaces. The men wore great turbans on their heads. The women decorated their ears with pearl rings, their necks with jewel lockets, their lips and eyes with different kinds of lipstick and ointment and their hands with large golden bangles. As they hastily passed over the stone road, the flower garlands decorating their bodies fell to the ground, and it appeared that a shower of flowers was falling from the sky. They approached the house of Nanda Maharaja with all sorts of gifts and blessed the child:

"Dear child, You will live long just to protect us."

While the cowherd women or *gopis,* as they are called, were blessing baby Krishna in this way, they offered a mixture of turmeric powder, oil, yogurt, milk and water. They sprinkled this mixture not only on the body of Krishna, but on everyone else too.

When the cowherd men saw the offerings of the cowherd women, they became even more joyful, and in response they began to throw yogurt, milk, clarified butter and water on the *gopis.* Then both parties began to throw butter on each other. Nanda Maharaja was also very happy to see the pastimes of the cowherd men and women. He gave charity to the different singers who were assembled there, some of whom were reciting important verses from the *Upanishads* and *Puranas,* some who were glorifying family ancestors, and some who were singing sweet songs. While Nanda Maharaja was worshiping Lord Vishnu, his only desire was that his newborn child, Krishna, should be happy and safe. But Nanda Maharaja did not realise that this child was the origin of the very same Vishnu he was praying to in order to protect his son.

Rohinidevi, the mother of Balarama, was the most fortunate wife of Vasudeva. She was away from her husband, yet when she heard of the birth of Krishna she dressed herself beautifully, just to congratulate Maharaja Nanda.

After the birth ceremony, Nanda Maharaja decided to go to Mathura to pay the annual tax to the government of Kamsa. Before leaving, he called for the able cowherd men of the village and asked them to take care of Vrindavana in his absence. Nanda Maharaja arrived in Mathura, and when Vasudeva got the news he came straight away to where Nanda was staying to warmly congratulate his friend. Anxious about his two sons, Krishna and Balarama, who had been put under the protection of Nanda without Nanda's knowledge, Vasudeva inquired about Them with great anxiety. As we know, Balarama had been transferred to the womb of Rohini, Vasudeva's own wife, who was kept under the protection of Nanda Maharaja. Krishna was personally delivered to Yashoda on that stormy night, and exchanged with her daughter, who then later appeared as the Goddess Durga before Kamsa. Although Nanda Maharaja knew that Balarama was the son of Vasudeva, he did not know that Krishna was also Vasudeva's son. But Vasudeva was aware of this fact, and hence his interest in both boys.

"My dear friend," Vasudeva said to Nanda, "I hope Krishna and Balarama are well. You know it is difficult for friends and family members to always live together. We are just like plants and creepers floating on the waves of the ocean. Sometimes they come together, and sometimes they separate forever: one plant goes one way, and another plant goes another. Similarly, our families may be happy whilst living together, but in the course of the waves of time, we must become separated." Even as Vasudeva spoke he knew he could not reveal the whole situation. "Please tell me about the welfare of Vrindavana," he enquired, "I feel sorry that I am not able to give protection to my own sons born of Devaki. Sometimes I feel all my good fortune is lost."

"My dear Vasudeva," Nanda Maharaja replied, "I know how aggrieved you are by the actions of your brother-in-law, the cruel king Kamsa, who has killed all your sons born of Devaki. Do not be upset; everyone is subject to his past deeds, and one who knows about the philosophy of karma, action and reaction, is a man in knowledge. Such a person will not be disturbed by any incident, happy or miserable, since he knows it is a direct result of whatever he has done in the past."

Vasudeva was grateful to hear his friend's advice, but he had some urgent advice to give too.

"My dear Nanda," Vasudeva said, "If you have already paid the government your taxes, then I advise you to return quickly to your home. I think there may soon be some disturbances in Gokula."

After saying this Vasudeva started out for his home. Nanda Maharaja bade him farewell, paid his taxes and then set out for home with the other cowherd men. As Nanda Maharaja was returning to Gokula, he thought carefully about Vasudeva's warning.

"There is some truth in it," he thought. Then out of fear he began to pray to the Supreme Personality of Godhead.

* * *

8. Putana Killed

"I hear you are an expert at killing small children; is this correct?" Kamsa asked the enormous, hideous hag, Putana, who stood before him.

"That is true my lord, I love killing defenceless children, and I am most expert in this black art," she replied with glee.

"Excellent, then you must go straight away and kill as many newborn children as you can. I want this Krishna dead," Kamsa ordered.

"It will give me great pleasure my lord." Saying this, the witch mounted the branch of a special type of tree and flew off into the night sky. (This black art of witchcraft is still practiced by some women in the remote northwestern part of India.)

Eventually Putana landed in Gokula, near the village of Vrindavana, and soon learned that a newborn child was present at the home of Nanda Maharaja. She changed her form to that of an extremely attractive woman and approached the house of mother Yashoda. As she walked through the streets to Nanda Maharaja's home, she glanced at everyone with a smiling face that captivated all the residents of Vrindavana. Because of her exquisite beauty, no one stopped her, and she freely entered the house of Nanda Maharaja. Putana, the killer of many, many children, found baby Krishna lying on a small bed, and she could at once perceive that the baby was hiding some amazing powers, just as fire is sometimes covered by ashes.

"This child is so powerful. He could destroy the whole universe, I must be careful," thought Putana as she looked down at the lovely blue form of baby Krishna.

Krishna behaved just like a small baby and closed His eyes. Before coming, Putana had smeared deadly poison on her milk filled breasts, and she now gently lifted Krishna out of His cot and onto her lap to feed Him. Both Yashoda and Rohini were present, but they thought nothing of it since she showed such motherly affection towards Krishna.

After taking the baby on her lap, Putana pushed her poisoned nipple into Krishna's rosy-lipped mouth. She was sure that as soon as He sucked her breast, He would die. But baby Krishna started sucking angrily with great force. He sucked so hard that Putana began to feel extreme pain.

"Oh, child, leave me, leave me!" Putana cried loudly as sweat poured off her body.

Everyone became alarmed at the sight of this beautiful woman screaming in pain as she tried to pull Krishna off her breast. Krishna sucked out not only the milk and poison, but her very life air too. As she yelled in agony she suddenly assumed her real, ugly form as a huge demon. She opened her fierce mouth and spread her arms and legs everywhere. The long hair on her head was scattered all over her body which had grown twelve miles high. Her huge frame crushed forests of trees as she came crashing to the ground with a shuddering thud. There was a tremendous vibration on the earth and in the sky, on the

upper and lower planets and in all directions, and people
thought that thunderbolts were falling from the heavens.
Everyone was amazed at the size of the gigantic witch.
Her teeth appeared just like ploughs, her nostrils like
mountain caves, her breasts like small hills, and her hair
was like a vast reddish bush. Her eye sockets appeared
like dark wells, her two thighs like the banks of a river, her
hands like two bridges, and her abdomen seemed like a
dried-up lake.

All the cowherd men and women were struck with awe
and wonder upon seeing this. When the *gopis* saw little
Krishna fearlessly playing on Putana's lap, they quickly
came and picked Him up. Mother Yashoda, Rohini and
other elder *gopis* then performed auspicious rituals by
walking a cow around little Krishna, washing Him with its
urine and sprinkling Him with the dust from its hooves,
after which they chanted the names of Vishnu. All this was
to give Krishna's body full protection from evil spirits and
ghosts. Sometimes such beings appear in dreams and
cause much fear, or as old women who suck the blood of
small children. But mother Yashoda was firmly convinced
that no such ghosts and evil spirits could remain where
there was chanting of the holy names of God. After saying
these mantras, mother Yashoda took Krishna and let Him
suck her own breast. Nanda Maharaja then remembered
Vasudeva's warning to him when they met in Mathura,
and realized he must be a great mystic, having foretold
the future so accurately. He had warned there would be
trouble, and sure enough he was right.

After this, all the residents of Vrindavana cut the gigantic body of Putana into pieces and piled it up with wood for burning. When all the limbs of Putana's body were burning, the smoke gave off a pleasing aroma due to her being killed by Krishna. The demon Putana was washed of all her sinful activities since she had come to offer milk to Krishna who had then directly taken her life. Because of this she was liberated and attained a spiritual body. This shows that devotional service to Krishna is so sublime that even a little, rendered knowingly or unknowingly, gives one the greatest transcendental benefit. If simply by offering something as an enemy, Putana got so much benefit, then who can measure the benefit of worshiping Him with love and affection? Therefore only Krishna should be worshiped, since so much benefit awaits the worshiper.

* * *

9. Krishna's Birthday

On Krishna's first birthday, Yashoda and Nanda Maharaja arranged for a celebration ceremony and invited all the cowherd men and women to come. Musicians played and all the learned *brahmanas* who were also invited chanted Vedic hymns for the good fortune of little Krishna. During the chanting, Krishna was bathed by mother Yashoda. This bathing ceremony is technically called *abhisheka*, and even today it is observed in all the temples of Vrindavana on Janmastami Day, or the birthday of Lord Krishna.

On this occasion mother Yashoda arranged to distribute a large quantity of grains. First-class cows, decorated with golden ornaments, were made ready to be given in charity to the learned, respectable *brahmanas*. Yashoda took her bath and dressed herself nicely, and taking child Krishna, who had also been dressed and bathed, on her lap, she sat down to hear the Vedic hymns chanted by the *brahmanas*. While she listened, the child appeared to be falling asleep, and therefore mother Yashoda silently laid Him down on a bed she had made up under the shade of a wooden cart. Being so engrossed in receiving all her friends, relatives and other residents of Vrindavana, she completely forgot to feed Krishna His milk. He was crying from hunger, but mother Yashoda could not hear Him due to all the noise. Krishna became angry, lifted His legs and began to kick His lotus feet just like an ordinary child. In so doing He kicked the wheel of the cart, causing it to collapse. Various utensils and dishes made of brass and other metals had been piled up in the handcart, and they all fell down with a great clatter. Krishna had kicked with such force that the wheel of the cart separated from the axle, and the spokes of the wheel were all broken and scattered all over the place. Mother Yashoda and all the *gopis*, as well as Maharaja Nanda and the cowherd men, were astonished as to how the cart could have collapsed by itself. Some small children, who had been left to play with baby Krishna, informed the crowd that it was due to Krishna's striking His feet against the wheel.

"How can you believe the statements of these children?" said one of the adults. The cowherd men and women could not understand that the all-powerful Personality of Godhead was lying right before their eyes as a baby, and that He could do anything. While the discussion was going on, baby Krishna cried. Mother Yashoda picked the child up on her lap and called the learned *brahmanas* to chant holy, Vedic hymns to counteract the evil spirits. At the same time she allowed the baby to suck her breast. After this, all the stronger cowherd men put the broken cart back together, and all the scattered pots and pans were set up as before. The *brahmanas* then began to make offerings to the sacrificial fire with yogurt, butter, *kusha* grass and water. They worshiped the Supreme Personality of Godhead for the good fortune of the child (unaware that the child was Himself the Supreme Personality of Godhead).

The *brahmanas* were all qualified because they were not envious, they always spoke the truth, they were never proud, they were non-violent, and they never claimed any false prestige. With firm faith in such qualified *brahmanas,* Nanda Maharaja took his child on his lap and bathed Him with water mixed with various herbs while the *brahmanas* chanted hymns from the *Rig, Yajur* and *Sama Vedas.*

Nanda Maharaja again gave huge quantities of grains and many cows to the *brahmanas.* All the cows given in charity were covered with gold-embroidered garments; their horns bedecked with golden rings; their hooves covered with silver plate and their necks draped with garlands of flowers.

* * *

10. The Whirlwind Demon

Shortly after the ceremony, when mother Yashoda was patting her baby on her lap, she noticed He felt much heavier than usual. He grew so heavy she could no longer hold Him, and so Yashoda reluctantly placed Him on the ground and went about her household affairs. At that time a demon named Trinavarta, under orders from Kamsa, appeared there in the form of a whirlwind. He picked the child up on his shoulders and raised a great dust storm all over Vrindavana, covering everyone's eyes. Within a few moments the whole area of Vrindavana became so densely dark that no one could see anything. When mother Yashoda could not see her baby anywhere she began to cry piteously and fell down on the ground. All the cowherd women immediately came and began to look for the baby, but they could not find Him.

Trinavarta spun high into the sky with Krishna on his shoulder, but the baby mysteriously became heavier and heavier as He clung to the demon's neck. Little Krishna became so heavy that Trinavarta began to slow down under the strain. Soon the baby was as heavy as a mountain and Trinavarta found he was unable to struggle out of His clutches. Then his eyes popped out from their sockets and he hurtled back down towards the ground, crying fiercely. Trinavarta's body smashed into a stone slab and he died instantly.

As the dust settled, the *gopis* saw that the terrible demon had been killed and that baby Krishna was happily playing on his body. They came and picked Krishna up with great affection. The cowherd men and women became very happy to get back their beloved child Krishna. They began to talk about how wonderful it was that the demon had taken away the child to devour Him but could not do so; instead he fell down dead. "This is no doubt because those who are too sinful die from their sinful reactions," they said, "and child Krishna is pious; therefore He is safe from all kinds of fearful situations."

After seeing what had happened, Nanda Maharaja thought of Vasudeva's words of warning again and again.

Once, when Yashoda was nursing her child and patting Him with great affection, there streamed a plentiful supply of milk from her breast. But when she opened His mouth with her fingers in order to feed Him, she observed something quite amazing. She saw within Krishna's mouth the entire universal manifestation, the whole sky, including the stars, the sun, moon, fire, air, seas, islands, mountains, rivers, forests and all other movable and immovable things. When mother Yashoda saw all this, her heart began to throb and she said to herself, "How amazing this is!" She could not express anything, but simply closed her eyes, absorbed in wonderful thoughts.

The Supreme Personality of Godhead is always the Supreme Personality of Godhead, whether He is manifested as a child on the lap of His mother or as a charioteer on the battlefield of Kurukshetra. The idea that one can become God by meditation or by some other material activity is clearly false. God is always God in any condition or status, and we, the living entities, are always His tiny parts and parcels. We can never be equal to the Supreme Personality of Godhead at any time, as some false religionists like to claim.

Vasudeva asked his family priest, Garga Muni, to visit Nanda Maharaja's home in order to astrologically calculate the future life of Krishna. Garga Muni was a great saintly sage who had undergone many austerities and penances and been appointed head priest of the Yadu dynasty. When he arrived, Nanda Maharaja was very pleased to see him and immediately stood up with folded hands and offered his respectful obeisances. He offered Garga Muni a comfortable sitting place and a warm reception.

"My dear *brahmana*," he said politely, "we are always engaged in household affairs and so keep forgetting our real duty, which is self-realization. Your appearance in my house is only to remind us of the true spiritual purpose of life. Other than this you have no purpose to visit householders like myself."

By his astrological calculation, Garga Muni could understand that Krishna was the son of Devaki but that He was being kept under the care of Nanda Maharaja, which Nanda did not know. Garga Muni warned Nanda Maharaja that if he publicly performed the name-giving ceremony, then Kamsa would come to learn that Krishna was really the son of Devaki and Vasudeva. So to avoid any dangerous and unwanted attention from Kamsa, Garga Muni performed the brahminical name-giving ceremony as secretly as possible in the cowshed of Nanda Maharaja. He informed

Nanda Maharaja that the son of Rohini would be very pleasing to His family members and relatives and that in the future He would be extraordinarily strong. Because of this great strength He would be called Balarama. Garga Muni was careful not to disclose the fact that Balarama also appeared in the womb of Devaki and was only subsequently transferred to the womb of Rohini. This meant that Krishna and Balarama were real brothers, both being originally sons of Devaki. Garga Muni then informed Nanda Maharaja:

"As far as your son is concerned, this child has taken different bodily complexions in different *yugas* [millennia]. First He assumed the colour white, then red, then yellow, and now He has assumed the colour blackish-blue. In fact this son has had many, many other names and activities due to His different pastimes. In His previous births this child many times protected righteous persons from the hands of rogues and thieves whenever there was great upheaval in human society. Your child is so powerful that anyone who becomes His devotee will never be troubled by enemies. Just as the *devatas* are always protected by Lord Vishnu, the devotees of your child will always be protected by Narayana, the Supreme Personality of Godhead. This child will grow in power, beauty, opulence—in everything—on the level of Narayana, the Supreme Personality of Godhead. Therefore I would advise that you protect Him carefully so that He may grow without disturbance." After giving all this information Garga Muni returned to his home.

Nanda Maharaja began to think of himself as the most fortunate person in the world to have such a wonderful son.

* * *

11. Two Naughty Boys

A short time after this incident, both Balarama and Krishna began to crawl on Their hands and knees, greatly pleasing Their mothers. The bells tied to Their waist and ankles sounded fascinating as They moved around most enchantingly. Sometimes, just like ordinary children, They would be frightened by others and would hurry to Their mothers for protection. Sometimes They would fall into the clay and mud of Vrindavana and would approach Their mothers covered in dirt. As soon as They came crawling to Their mothers, Yashoda and Rohini would take Them on their laps and, covering Them with the lower portion of their *saris*, allow Them to suck their breasts. When the babies were sucking their breasts, the mothers would see small teeth coming through, which gave them great joy as they watched their babies grow. Sometimes the naughty babies would crawl up to the cowshed, catch the tail of a calf and stand up. The calves, being disturbed, would begin running here and there, and the children would be dragged over clay and cow dung. To see this fun, Yashoda and Rohini would call all their neighbouring friends, the *gopis*. Upon seeing these childhood pastimes of Lord Krishna, the *gopis* would be merged in transcendental bliss and in their enjoyment would laugh loudly.

Both Krishna and Balarama were so restless that Their mothers would try to protect Them from cows, bulls, monkeys, water, fire and birds while they were working around the house. Always anxious to protect the children, they were never completely tranquil. In a short time, both Krishna and Balarama began to stand up and totter on Their legs. When Krishna and Balarama began to walk, other friends of the same age joined Them.

All the *gopi* friends of Yashoda and Rohini enjoyed the naughty childish activities of Krishna and Balarama in Vrindavana. In order to enjoy further transcendental bliss, they all assembled and went to mother Yashoda to lodge complaints against the restless boys. When Krishna was sitting before mother Yashoda, the elder *gopis* began to complain thus:

"Dear Yashoda, why don't you restrict your naughty Krishna? He comes to our houses along with Balarama every morning and evening, and before the milking of the cows, They let loose the calves, and the calves drink all the milk of the cows, so when we go to milk the cows, we find no milk, and we have to return with empty pots. If we warn Krishna and Balarama about doing this, They simply smile so charmingly that we cannot do anything. Also, your Krishna and Balarama find great pleasure in stealing our stock of yogurt and butter from wherever we keep it. When Krishna and Balarama are caught stealing the yogurt and butter, They say: "Why do you accuse Us of stealing? Do you think that butter and yogurt are scarce in Our house?" Sometimes They steal butter, yogurt and milk and distribute them to the monkeys. When the monkeys are well fed and do not take any more, then your boys chide, 'This milk and butter and yogurt are useless—even the monkeys won't take it.' And They break the pots and throw them hither and thither. If we keep our stock of yogurt, butter and milk in a solitary, dark place, your Krishna and Balarama still find it by the glaring effulgence of the ornaments and jewels on Their bodies. If by chance They cannot find the hidden butter and yogurt, They go to our little babies and pinch their bodies so that they cry, and then They go away. If we keep our stock of butter and yogurt hanging on a swing high on the ceiling, out of the reach of these naughty boys, They somehow still manage to reach it by piling up wooden planks over the grinding stone. And if They cannot reach, They make a hole in the pot. We think therefore that you'd better take all the jewelled ornaments from the bodies of your children."

On hearing this, Yashoda would agree saying: "All right, I will take all the jewels from Krishna so that He cannot see the butter hidden in the darkness."

"No, no, don't do this." The *gopis* would say, "What good will you do by taking away the jewels? We do not know what kind of boys these are, but even without ornaments They spread some kind of light so that even in darkness They can see everything."

"All right," mother Yashoda would say, "keep your butter and yogurt carefully so that They may not reach it."

"Yes, actually we do so, but because we are sometimes engaged in our household duties, these naughty boys enter our house somehow or other and spoil everything. Sometimes, being unable to steal our butter and yogurt, out of anger They pass urine on the clean floor and sometimes spit on it. Now just see how your boy is hearing these complaints. All day He simply makes arrangements to steal our butter and yogurt, and now He is just sitting silently like a good little boy. Just see His face."

When mother Yashoda thought to chastise her son after hearing all the complaints, she saw His pitiable face and could not chastise Him, but smiled at Him instead.

Another day, when Krishna and Balarama were playing with Their friends, all the boys joined Balarama and complained to mother Yashoda that Krishna had eaten clay. On hearing this, mother Yashoda caught hold of Krishna's hand and said:

"My dear Krishna, why have You eaten earth in a solitary place? Just see, all Your friends, including Balarama, are complaining about You." Being afraid of His mother, Krishna replied:

"My dear mother, all these boys, including My elder brother, Balarama, are speaking lies against Me. I have never eaten any clay. My elder brother, Balarama, while playing with Me today, became angry, and therefore He has joined with the other boys to complain against Me. They have all ganged up so you will be angry and chastise Me. If you want you can look in My mouth to see whether I have eaten clay or not."

"All right, if You are telling the truth then just open Your mouth and I shall see," His mother replied.

Krishna opened His mouth just like an ordinary boy. Then, just as she did previously, mother Yashoda saw within that mouth the complete opulence of creation. She saw the entire outer space in all directions, mountains, islands, oceans, seas, planets, air, fire, moon and stars.

Along with the moon and the stars she also saw all the elements—everything necessary for the universe to exist. She also saw herself taking Krishna on her lap and having Him suck her breast. Upon seeing all this, she became struck with awe and began to wonder whether she was dreaming or actually seeing something extraordinary. She concluded that she was either dreaming or seeing the play of the illusory energy of the Supreme Personality of Godhead. She thought that she had become mad, mentally deranged, to see all those things. Then she thought, "It may be some sort of cosmic, mystic power attained by my child, and therefore I am perplexed by such visions within His mouth. Let me offer my respectful obeisances to the Supreme Personality of Godhead and pray that He will always protect me."

While mother Yashoda was thinking such thoughts, Lord Krishna, through his mystic powers, covered her once more with maternal affection. Immediately mother Yashoda forgot all those thoughts about her son, and she again accepted Krishna as her own little child. She took Him on her lap and became overwhelmed with motherly love.

* * *

12. Mother Yashoda Binds Lord Krishna

Once, seeing that her maidservant was busy with other duties, mother Yashoda personally took charge of churning butter. While she worked, she sang the childhood pastimes of Krishna and enjoyed thinking of her son. The end of her *sari* was tightly wrapped while she churned, and on account of her intense love for her son, milk automatically dripped from her breasts. The bangles and bracelets on her hands tinkled as they touched each other, and her earrings and breasts shook. There were drops of perspiration on her face, and the flower garland which was on her head scattered here and there. Before this lovely sight, Lord Krishna appeared as a child. He felt hungry, and to increase His mother's love, He wanted her to stop churning. He made it clear that her first business was to let Him suck her breast, and that she could churn butter later.

Mother Yashoda took her son on her lap and pushed the nipple of her breast into His mouth, and while Krishna was sucking the milk, she was smiling, enjoying the beauty of her child's face. Suddenly, the milk which was on the stove began to boil over. Mother Yashoda at once put Krishna aside and went to the stove. Left in that state by His mother, Krishna became angry, and His lips and eyes became red in rage. He pressed His teeth and lips, and taking up a piece of stone, He broke the butter pot. He took butter out of it, and with false tears in His eyes, He began to eat it in a secluded place.

In the meantime, mother Yashoda returned to the churning place after setting the overflowing milk pan in order. She saw the broken pot in which the churning yogurt had been kept. Since she could not find her boy, she concluded that the broken pot was His work. She smiled as she thought, "The child is very clever. After breaking the pot He has left this place, fearing punishment." After she looked all over, she eventually found Him sitting on a big wooden grinding mortar which was kept upside down. He was taking butter from a pot which was hanging from the ceiling on a swing, and He was feeding it to the monkeys. She saw Krishna looking this way and that way in fear of her, being fully aware of His own naughty behaviour. She silently approached Him from behind. Krishna, however, saw her coming toward Him with a stick in her hand, and He quickly got down from the grinding mortar and began to run away in fear. Mother Yashoda chased Him everywhere, trying to catch the Supreme Personality of Godhead. Mother Yashoda could not easily catch the fast-running child and as she chased Him, the flowers in her hair fell to the ground. Although she was tired, she somehow reached her naughty child and captured Him. When He was caught, Krishna was almost at the point of crying and He smeared His hands over His eyes, which were anointed with black eye cosmetics. The child saw His mother's face while she stood over Him, and His eyes became restless from fear.

Mother Yashoda could see that Krishna was

unnecessarily afraid. Being the topmost well-wisher of her child, mother Yashoda thought, "If the child is too fearful of me, I don't know what will happen to Him." She then threw away her stick. In order to punish Him she decided to tie His hands with some ropes. She did not know it, but it was actually impossible for her to bind the Supreme Personality of Godhead without His sanction. Mother Yashoda was thinking that Krishna was her tiny child; she did not know that He had no limitation. Indeed, Krishna is unlimited and all-pervading and is Himself the whole universe. Still, mother Yashoda was thinking of Krishna as her child so she tried to tie Him to a wooden grinding mortar; only the rope she was using appeared to be too short—by two inches. She gathered more ropes from the house and added to it, but still she found the same shortage. In this way, she connected all the ropes available at home, but when the final knot was added, she saw that it was still two inches too short. Mother Yashoda was smiling, but astonished. How was it happening?

In attempting to bind her son, she became tired. Then Lord Krishna appreciated the hard labour of His mother, and being compassionate upon her, allowed Himself to be bound by her ropes. Krishna, playing as a human child in the house of mother Yashoda, was performing His own selected pastimes. Of course, no one can control the Supreme Personality of Godhead, but the Lord feels transcendental pleasure by giving Himself to the protection of His devotee.

After binding her son, mother Yashoda went back to her household affairs. At that time, bound up to the wooden mortar, Krishna could see a pair of *arjuna* trees before Him. Lord Sri Krishna thought to Himself, "Mother Yashoda first left without feeding Me sufficient milk, and therefore I broke the pot of yogurt and distributed the butter in charity to the monkeys. Now she has bound Me up to a wooden mortar. So I shall do something more mischievous than before." And thus He thought of pulling down the two tall *arjuna* trees.

* * *

13. The Twin Arjuna Trees

There is an interesting history behind this pair of *arjuna* trees. There were once two great *devatas* named Nalakuvara and Manigreeva who were sons of the treasurer of the *devatas*, Kuvera, who was a great devotee of Lord Shiva. By the grace of Lord Shiva, Kuvera's material opulences had no limit. As a rich man's sons often become addicted to wine and women, so these two sons of Kuvera were also addicted to such things. Once, these two brothers entered the garden of Lord Shiva in the province of Kailasha on the bank of the Mandakini Ganges. There they drank much and listened to the sweet singing of beautiful women who accompanied them in that garden of fragrant flowers. In an intoxicated condition, they both entered the water of the Ganges, which was full with lotus flowers, and there they began to enjoy the company of the young girls.

While they were enjoying themselves in the water, all of a sudden Narada Muni happened to pass that way. As Narada glanced in their direction he could understand that Nalakuvara and Manigreeva were too intoxicated to even notice him since they carried on cavorting without their clothes on. However, the young girls were not so intoxicated and at once became shy before the great sage Narada. On seeing the two *devatas'* behaviour Narada decided to be merciful and curse them.

He wanted to finish their false enjoyment and put them into a condition where they could not be so proud of their material opulence, beauty and prestige; and so he decided the best punishment for them was to turn them into trees. He also arranged that, although having the bodies of trees, they would keep their memory and be fully aware of why they were being punished. Sage Narada therefore thought that the two brothers should remain for one hundred *devata* years, in the form of trees, and after that they would be fortunate enough to see the Supreme Personality of Godhead face to face. Thus they would become great devotees of the Lord.

After this, the great sage Narada returned to his abode, known as Narayanashrama, and the two *devatas* turned into the twin *arjuna* trees growing in Nanda's courtyard.

Although child Krishna was bound up to the wooden mortar, He began to crawl towards these same two trees in order to fulfil the prophecy of His great devotee Narada made thousands of years previously. Lord Krishna knew that the trees standing before Him were actually the sons of Kuvera.

"I must now fulfil the words of My great devotee Narada," He thought. Then He proceeded through the passage between the two trees. Although He was able to pass through the passage, the large wooden mortar stuck horizontally between the trees. Taking advantage of this, with great strength Lord Krishna began to pull the rope, which was tied to the mortar. As soon as He pulled, the two trees fell down with a great crash. Out of the broken, fallen trees came the two great personalities, shining like blazing fire. The two purified personalities then came before Krishna and bowed down to offer their respects and prayers in the following words:

"Dear Lord Krishna, You are the original Personality of Godhead, master of all mystic powers. Learned *brahmanas* know very well that this universe is an expansion of Your powers. You are the eternal God, Lord Vishnu, who is all-pervading, the imperishable controller of everything, and You are eternal time." After this, the *devatas* circled the Lord many times, bowed down before Him again and again, and then left.

Hearing the crashing sound, Nanda Maharaja along with all the inhabitants of Gokula, ran quickly to the spot and were astonished to see how the two great trees had suddenly fallen for no apparent reason. They saw Krishna was bound up to the wooden mortar by the ropes of mother Yashoda, and so they thought that the destruction must have been caused by a demon of some sort. Otherwise, how was it possible? At the same time, they were disturbed that such strange things were always happening to Krishna. While the cowherd men were trying to understand what had happened, the small children who were playing there informed the men that the trees had fallen because Krishna had pulled the wooden mortar with the rope binding Him.

"Krishna came in between the two trees," they explained, "and the wooden mortar fell on its side and stuck in between the trees. Krishna pulled the rope, and the trees fell down. When the trees fell down, two dazzling men came out of them, and they said something to Krishna."

Most of the cowherd men did not believe the children, but those who did told Nanda Maharaja:

"Your child is different from all other children. He just might have done it."

Nanda Maharaja smiled on hearing about the extraordinary abilities of his son. He came forward and untied the rope and released Krishna. After being freed by Nanda Maharaja, Krishna was taken onto the laps of the elder *gopis.* They took Him away to the courtyard of the house and began to clap, praising His wonderful activities. Krishna danced along with their clapping, just like an ordinary child. The Supreme Lord Krishna, being completely controlled by the *gopis*, sang and danced just like a puppet in their hands.

* * *

14. The Fruit Seller

Sometimes mother Yashoda used to ask Krishna to bring a wooden plank for her to sit on. Although the wooden plank was too heavy to be carried by a child, still, somehow or other Krishna would bring it to His mother. Sometimes, while worshiping Narayana, His father would ask Him to bring his wooden slippers, and Krishna, with great difficulty, would put the slippers on His head and bring them to His father. The Lord was exhibiting such childish dealings with the inhabitants of Vrindavana because He wanted to show the great philosophers and sages searching after the Absolute Truth how the Supreme Personality of Godhead, the Absolute Truth, is controlled by and subject to the desires of His pure devotees.

One day, a fruit seller came before the house of Nanda Maharaja calling;

"If anyone wants fruits please come and take them from me!" In those days exchange was by barter; therefore Krishna may have seen His parents acquire fruits and other things by bartering grains. Krishna picked up a handful of grains and went to exchange them for some fruits, but since His palms were small, and He was not careful to hold them tightly, He dropped most of them on the floor. The fruit vendor saw this and was completely captivated by the beauty of the Lord. She accepted whatever few grains were left in His palm and filled His hands with ripened fruits. When she next looked down at her fruit basket she saw it had mysteriously become filled with glittering jewels. This shows that if someone gives something to the Lord he does not lose anything, but gains by a million times.

One day Lord Krishna was playing with Balarama and the other children on the bank of the Yamuna river, and because it was already late, Rohini, the mother of Balarama, went to call them back home. But Balarama and Krishna were so engrossed in playing with Their friends that They did not wish to come back. Unable to take Them with her, Rohini returned home alone and sent mother Yashoda to call Them again. Mother Yashoda was so affectionate toward her son that as soon as she came out to call Him back home, her breast filled up with milk. She loudly cried:

"My dear child, please come back home. Your time for lunch is already past." She then said, "My dear Krishna, O my dear lotus-eyed child, please come and suck my breast. You have played enough. You must be so hungry, my dear little child. You must be tired from playing for so long." She also addressed Balarama thus: "My dear Balarama please come back with Your younger brother Krishna immediately. You have been playing since morning, and You must be very tired. Please come back and take Your lunch at home. Your father Nandaraja is waiting for You. He has to eat, so You must come back so that he can eat."

As soon as Krishna and Balarama heard that Nanda Maharaja was waiting for Them and could not eat his food in Their absence, They started to return. Their playmates complained, "Krishna is leaving us just when we were having most fun. Next time we shall not allow Him to leave."

His playmates then threatened not to allow Him to play with them again. Krishna became afraid, and instead of going back home, He went back again to play with the boys. At that time, mother Yashoda scolded the children and told Krishna:

"My dear Krishna, do You think that You are a street boy who has no home? I see Your body has become very dirty from playing since morning. Now come home and take Your bath. Besides, today is Your birthday ceremony; therefore You should come back home and give cows in charity to the *brahmanas*. Don't You see how Your playmates are decorated with ornaments by their mothers? You should also be cleansed and decorated with nice clothes and ornaments and then later You may go on playing."

When Krishna and Balarama, finally came home, she bathed Them and dressed Them with ornaments. Mother Yashoda then called for the *brahmanas,* and through her children she gave many cows in charity for the occasion of Krishna's birthday.

* * *

15. Leaving for Vrindavana Forest

The elderly cowherd men met one day to discuss how they could put a stop to all the terrible disturbances that had come since Krishna's appearance. At the meeting Upananda, the brother of Nanda Maharaja, said:

"My dear friends! We should leave this forest of Mahavana for another place because great demons keep coming here trying to kill the small children. Just consider what happened with that witch, Putana and Krishna. Next the whirlwind demon took Krishna away in the sky, but by the grace of the Lord once again He was saved. Very recently, this child was playing between two trees which fell down violently, and the Lord saved Him yet again. Just imagine the calamity if this child or any other child playing with Him were crushed by the falling trees! Considering all these incidents, we must conclude that this place is no longer safe. I think that we should all go to the forest known as Vrindavana, where just now there are newly grown plants and herbs. It is a perfect pasturing ground for our cows, and we and our families can live there peacefully."

All the cowherd men agreed with Upananda. "Yes, let us immediately go there." Everyone then loaded all their household furniture and utensils on the carts and prepared to go to Vrindavana. All the old men of the village, the children and the women were arranged on seats, and the cowherd men equipped themselves with bows and arrows

to follow the carts. All the cows and bulls were placed in
the front along with their calves, while the men, with their
bows and arrows, surrounded the herds and carts and
began to blow on their horns and bugles. In this way, with
a tumultuous sound, they started for Vrindavana.

And who can describe the damsels of Vraja (*gopis*)?
They were all seated on the carts and were beautifully
dressed with ornaments and costly *saris*. As usual they
chanted the pastimes of child Krishna. Mother Yashoda
and mother Rohini were seated on a separate cart with
Krishna and Balarama on their laps. While mother Rohini
and Yashoda were riding on the cart, they talked to Krishna
and Balarama, and feeling the pleasure of such talks, they
looked most beautiful.

In this way, after reaching Vrindavana they drew all the
carts together in a half circle, and in this way constructed
a temporary residence. When Krishna and Balarama saw
the beautiful appearance of Vrindavana, Govardhana Hill
and the banks of the river Yamuna, They felt very happy.
As They grew up They began talking with Their parents
and others in childish language, and thus They gave great
pleasure to all the inhabitants of Vrindavana.

Soon Krishna and Balarama had grown sufficiently to
be given charge of the calves. From the very beginning of
their childhood, cowherd boys are trained to take care of
the cows, and their first responsibility is to take care of the
little calves. So, along with the other little cowherd boys,
Krishna and Balarama went into the pasturing ground and
took charge of the calves, and played with Their friends.
While looking after the calves, sometimes the two brothers

played on Their flutes and sometimes They played with *amalaka* and *bael* fruits, just as small children play with balls. Sometimes They danced and made tinkling sounds with Their ankle bells. Sometimes They made Themselves into bulls and cows by covering Themselves with blankets. Thus Krishna and Balarama played. The two brothers also used to imitate the sounds of bulls and cows and play at bullfighting. Sometimes They used to imitate the sounds of various animals and birds. In this way, They enjoyed Their childhood pastimes seemingly like ordinary children.

* * *

16. Killing the Demons Vatsasura and Bakasura

Once, when Krishna and Balarama were playing on the bank of the Yamuna, a demon called Vatsasura assumed the shape of a calf and came there to kill them. By taking the shape of a calf the demon thought he could mingle unnoticed with the other calves. However, Krishna noticed him straight away and told Balarama; then both brothers silently approached him. Krishna suddenly caught hold of the demon-calf by the two hind legs and tail, whipped him around forcibly and threw him up into a tree. The demon lost his life and fell down from the top of the tree to the ground with a thud. When the demon lay dead on the ground, all the playmates of Krishna congratulated Him, "Well done, well done," and the *devatas* in the sky showered flowers with great satisfaction. In this way Krishna and Balarama enjoyed Their childhood pastimes as cowherd boys in Vrindavana.

One day, all the cowherd boys went to the bank of the river Yamuna to water their calves. When the calves drank water from the Yamuna, the boys also drank. After drinking, and when they were all sitting on the bank of the river, they saw a huge animal which looked something like an enormous heron. They all became afraid of this beast which was called Bakasura, and who was another evil friend of Kamsa. He immediately attacked Krishna with his pointed, sharp beak and quickly swallowed Him up. Seeing Krishna being swallowed, all the boys, headed by Balarama, became almost breathless with fear, as if they had died. As the Bakasura demon was swallowing Krishna, he suddenly felt a burning, fiery sensation in his throat. This was due to the glowing effulgence of Krishna. The demon quickly threw Krishna up and tried to kill Him by pinching Him in his beak. Bakasura did not know that although Krishna was playing the part of a child of Nanda Maharaja, He was still the original father of Lord Brahma, the creator of the universe. Krishna caught hold of the great gigantic heron by both the edges of his beak and pulled his mouth in two, just as a child easily splits a blade of grass. From the sky, the denizens of the heavenly planets showered fragrant flowers like the *mallika* as a token of their congratulations. Accompanying the showers of flowers was a vibration of bugles, drums and conchshells.

When the boys saw the showering of flowers and heard the celestial sounds, they became struck with wonder. And when they saw Krishna freed from the mouth of the great demon Bakasura, all of them, including Balarama, were so pleased that it seemed as if they had regained their very source of life. As soon as they saw Krishna coming towards them, they one after another embraced the son of Nanda and held Him to their chests. After this, they rounded up all the calves under their charge and began to return home.

When they arrived home, they spoke of the wonderful activities of the son of Nanda. When the *gopis* and cowherd men heard the story from the boys, they felt great happiness because naturally they loved Krishna, and by hearing about His glories and victorious activities they became still more affectionate toward Him. Thinking that child Krishna had been saved from the mouth of death, they looked upon His face with great love and affection. Indeed, they could not turn their faces from the vision of Krishna. The *gopis* and the men began to converse amongst themselves about how wonderful it was that child Krishna had been attacked in so many ways and so many times by so many demons, and yet the demons themselves had been killed and Krishna had remained uninjured. They were so absorbed in those talks about Krishna that they forgot all about the miseries of this world. This is the effect of Krishna consciousness. What was enjoyed five thousand years ago by Nanda Maharaja can still be enjoyed by persons who are in Krishna consciousness simply by talking about the transcendental pastimes of Krishna and His associates.

* * *

17. The Aghasura Demon

Balarama and Krishna used to play happily with their friends almost every day, sometimes imitating Lord Ramachandra's monkeys, who constructed the bridge over the Indian ocean, and Hanuman, who jumped over the water to Lanka to find Sita. Once the Lord desired to go early in the morning with all His cowherd boyfriends to the forest, where they were to meet and have lunch. As soon as He got up from bed, He blew His buffalo-horn bugle and called all His friends together. Keeping the calves before them, they started for the forest in a great procession. In this way, Lord Krishna assembled thousands of His boyfriends. They were each equipped with a stick, flute and horn, as well as a lunch bag. Each of them took care of thousands of calves. The jolly boys began to pick up flowers, leaves, twigs, peacock feathers and red clay from different places in the forest and further decorate themselves in different ways. While passing through the forest, one boy stole another boy's lunch package and passed it to a third. And when the boy whose lunch package was stolen came to know of it, he tried to take it back. But the boy who had it threw it to another boy and all of them joined in the fun.

When Lord Krishna went ahead to a see a particular place or some scenery in the distance, the boys behind Him ran to try to catch up and be the first to touch Him. So there was a great competition. One would say, "I will go there and touch Krishna," and another would say, "Oh, you cannot go. I'll touch Krishna first." Some of them played on their flutes or vibrated bugles made of buffalo horn. Some of them gladly followed the peacocks and imitated the sounds of the cuckoo. While the birds were flying in the sky, the boys ran after the birds' shadows along the ground and tried to follow their exact courses. Some of them went to the monkeys and silently sat down next to them, and others imitated the dancing of the peacocks. Some of them caught the tails of the monkeys and played with them, and when the monkeys jumped into a tree, the boys followed. When a monkey showed its face and teeth, a boy imitated and showed his teeth to the monkey. Some of the boys played with the frogs on the bank of the Yamuna, and when, out of fear, the frogs jumped into the water, the boys immediately dove in after them. They would also go to an empty well and make loud sounds, and when the echo came back, they would call it ill names and laugh.

When Lord Krishna was enjoying His childhood pastimes with His boyfriends, a demon named Aghasura approached them. He had also been sent by Kamsa and could not tolerate seeing Krishna play so happily, since he was the younger brother of Putana and Bakasura. He thought to himself, "Krishna has killed my brother and sister. Now I shall kill Him along with all His friends and calves." This Aghasura was so dangerous that even the denizens of heaven were afraid of him and were wondering, "When will this demon be killed?" On the other hand, the boys who were playing with Krishna had no fear of the demons. Aghasura thought that if he were to kill Krishna and all the cowherd boys, then automatically all the inhabitants of Vrindavana would die of grief.

Aghasura then expanded himself by the yogic ability called *mahima*. Demons are often expert in all kinds of mystic powers and Aghasura was able to expand himself up to eight miles and assume the shape of a fat serpent. Having attained this wonderful body, he stretched his mouth open in order to swallow all the boys, along with Krishna and Balarama, and sat on the path waiting for them to come.

Aghasura expanded his lips from land to sky; his lower lip was touching the ground, and his upper lip was touching the clouds. His jaws appeared like a big mountain cave, without limitation, and his teeth appeared just like mountain summits. His tongue appeared to be a broad road, his breathing was just like a hurricane and his eyes were blazing like fire. At first the boys thought that the demon was a statue, but after examining it they saw it for what it was. The boys began to talk among themselves:

"Dear friends, this appears to be a large creature, and he is lying in such a position just to swallow us all. Just see—is it not a big snake that has widened his mouth to eat all of us?"

Another boy said, "Yes, what you say is true. That fishy, bad odour coming from his mouth is the smell of his intestines."

Another boy said: "If we all enter the mouth of this great serpent together, how could it possibly swallow all of us? And even if it did, it could never swallow Krishna. Krishna

would immediately kill him, just as He did Bakasura."
Talking in this way, all the boys looked at the beautiful lotus
like face of Krishna, and they began to clap and smile.
And so they marched forward and entered the mouth of
the gigantic serpent.

The demon was waiting for Krishna to enter his mouth
so he could kill Him.

"Everyone has now entered except Krishna, who has
killed my brother and sister," Aghasura thought to himself.

When Krishna saw that His friends were lying within
the belly of a great serpent, He became momentarily upset.
He was also struck with wonder at how His external energy
works so wonderfully. He then began to consider how He
could kill the demon and at the same time save the boys
and calves. Finally, after some thought, He also entered
the mouth of the demon. When Krishna entered, all the
devatas, who had gathered to see the fun and who were
hiding within the clouds, expressed their feelings with the
words "Alas! Alas!" At the same time, all the friends of
Aghasura, especially Kamsa, expressed their joy. Krishna
began to expand Himself within the throat of the demon,
choking him to death. Aghasura's big eyes moved violently,
and he quickly suffocated. His life air burst out of a hole in
the upper part of his skull and the demon's spirit soul came
out like a dazzling light, illuminating all directions. After
the demon died, Krishna brought all the boys and calves
back to consciousness with His transcendental glance
alone, and they all came safely out of the mouth of the
demon. As soon as Krishna came out of the serpent's
mouth, the brightly glittering spirit soul of Aghasura merged

into His body. When the *devatas* saw this they became overwhelmed with joy and worshiped Krishna by showering Him with flowers. The residents of heaven danced in jubilation, and all the devotees of the Lord chanted the words *"Jaya! Jaya!* All glories to the Supreme Personality of Godhead!"

When Lord Brahma heard that singing, which resounded throughout the higher planetary system, he swiftly came down to see what had happened. Aghasura was certainly a most sinful living entity, and it is not possible for the sinful to enter the spiritual world. But in this particular case, because Krishna entered into Aghasura's body, the demon became fully cleansed of all his sinful reactions. Persons constantly thinking of the eternal form of the Lord in the shape of the Deity, or a form in their minds, are awarded the transcendental benediction of entering into the kingdom of God and associating with the Supreme Personality of Godhead.

The gigantic mouth of the demon remained in an open position for many days and gradually dried up; from then on the cowherd boys used it as a place to play and have fun. The killing of Aghasura took place when Krishna and all His boyfriends were under five years old. For one year there was no discussion of this incident in the village of Vraja (Vrindavana). It was not until a whole year later, when the boys were six that they told their parents of this wonderful adventure, and in the following chapter we find out why it took them so long.

* * *

18. The Stealing of the
Boys and Calves

After saving His friends from the mouth of Aghasura and killing the demon, Lord Krishna brought His friends to the bank of the Yamuna and addressed them as follows:

"My dear friends just see how this spot is so perfect for taking lunch and playing on the soft, sandy bank of the Yamuna. You can see how the lotus flowers in the water are beautifully blown and how they send their fragrance all around. The chirping of the birds along with cooing peacocks, surrounded by the whispering of the leaves in the trees, all combine and present sounds that echo one another. And this just enriches the beautiful scenery created by the trees here. Let us have our lunch in this spot because it is already late and we are hungry. Let the calves remain near us, and let them drink water from the Yamuna and eat the soft grasses."

On hearing Krishna's idea, all the boys became glad and said: "Certainly, let us all sit down here to take our lunch." They then let loose the calves to eat the soft grass. Sitting down on the ground and keeping Krishna in the centre, they began to open their lunch boxes which they had brought from home. Lord Sri Krishna was seated in the centre of the circle, and all the boys kept their faces toward Him. They ate and constantly enjoyed seeing the Lord face to face. Krishna appeared to be the whorl of a lotus flower, and the boys surrounding Him were like its petals. The boys collected flowers, leaves and tree bark and placed their lunch on them, and thus they began to eat, keeping company with Krishna. While taking lunch, each boy began to manifest different kinds of relations with Krishna, and they enjoyed each other's company with joking words.

While Lord Krishna was enjoying lunch with His friends, His flute was pushed within the belt of His cloth on His right side, and His bugle and cane were pushed in on the left-hand side. In his left palm He was holding a lump of food prepared with yogurt, butter, rice and pieces of fruit salad, which could be seen through His petal like fingers. The Supreme Personality of Godhead was laughing and joking, enjoying lunch with His friends in Vrindavana. At that time, the calves that were pasturing nearby entered into the deep forest, allured by new grasses, and gradually went out of sight. When the boys saw that the calves were not nearby, they became afraid for their safety, and they immediately cried out, "Krishna!" Since Krishna is the killer of fear personified, when they called out His name the boys at once rose above that fearful situation. With great affection Krishna said to His friends:

"My dear friends, you need not interrupt your lunch. Go on enjoying. I will go personally to find the calves." Thus Lord Krishna, still carrying the lump of yogurt-and-rice preparation in His left hand, started to search out the calves in the caves and bushes. He searched in the mountain and in the forests, but nowhere could He find them.

At the time when Aghasura was killed and the *devatas*

were looking on the incident with great surprise, Brahma, who was born out of the lotus flower growing out of the navel of Vishnu, also came to see. He was surprised how a little boy like Krishna could act so wonderfully. Although he was informed that the little cowherd boy was the Supreme Personality of Godhead, he wanted to see more of the Lord's glorious pastimes, and thus he stole all the calves and cowherd boys and took them to a different place. Lord Krishna searched for them along the bank of the Yamuna, where they had been taking their lunch together earlier; He thought: "Brahma has taken away all the boys and calves. How can I return alone to Vrindavana? Their mothers will be so upset!"

For the sake of his friends' mothers, as well as to convince Brahma of His supremacy, He immediately expanded Himself into the many forms of all the cowherd boys and calves. In the *Vedas* it is said that the Supreme Personality of Godhead has already expanded Himself into so many living entities by His energy. We are all expansions of this divine energy. Therefore it was not difficult for Him to expand Himself into many boys and calves. He expanded Himself to become exactly like the boys, who all had different facial and bodily features, who all spoke and behaved differently and who all wore different clothing and ornaments. He also expanded himself into the exact shape and size of every single calf.

In the *Vishnu Purana* it is said, *parasya brahmanah shaktih.* Whatever we can see in the cosmic manifestation—be it dull matter or the activities of the living entities—it is all simply an expansion of the energies of

the Lord, just as heat and light are the different expansions
of fire. Thus expanding Himself into thousands of calves
and boys, and surrounded by all these expansions of
Himself, Krishna entered the village of Vrindavana. The
villagers had no idea what had happened and as the calves
went to their cowsheds, and the boys went to their mothers
and homes, everything seemed quite normal.

The mothers of the boys heard the sound of their flutes
as they approached, and they came out of their homes
and embraced them. All the boys dealt with their mothers
as usual, and the mothers also bathed their children,
decorated them with *tilaka* (yellow clay from the Ganges),
ornaments and gave them something to eat after their day's
work. The cows, who were away in the pasturing ground,
returned in the evening and also called for their respective
calves. The calves quickly came to their mothers who
began to lick their bodies. Actually the cows' affection for
their calves and the elder *gopis'* affection for the boys
increased day by day, even though the calves and boys
were not their actual offspring. For one whole year,
continuously, Krishna expanded Himself as the calves and
cowherd boys.

Just before a year had passed, Krishna and Balarama
were looking after the calves in the forest when They saw
some cows grazing on the top of Govardhana Hill. The
cows could see down into the valley where the calves were
being taken care of by the boys. Suddenly, on sighting
their calves, the cows began to run towards them. They
leaped downhill with joined front and rear legs. The cows
were so melted with affection for their calves that they did

not care about the rough path from the top of Govardhana Hill down to the pasturing ground. They approached the calves with their milk bags full of milk and with raised tails. When they were coming down the hill, their milk bags were pouring milk on the ground out of intense motherly affection for the calves, although they were not their own calves. There appeared to be a great bond of affection between the cows and calves. When the cows were running down from the top of Govardhana Hill, the men who were taking care of them tried to stop them. Older cows are taken care of by the men, and the calves are taken care of by the boys; and as far as possible, the calves are kept separate from the cows, so that the calves do not drink all the available milk. Therefore the men who were taking care of the cows on the top of Govardhana Hill tried to stop them, but they failed. Baffled by their failure, they were feeling ashamed and angry; but when they came down and saw what they thought was their children taking care of the calves, they all of a sudden became very affectionate toward the children. It was quite astonishing. Although the men came down the hill baffled and angry, as soon as they saw their own children, their hearts melted with great affection, and their anger and unhappiness disappeared. They began to show fatherly love for the children, and with great affection they lifted them in their arms and embraced them. They began to smell their children's heads and enjoy their company with great happiness. After embracing their children, the men took the cows back to the top of Govardhana Hill. Along the way they began to think of their children, and affectionate tears fell from their eyes.

When Balarama saw this extraordinary exchange of affection between the cows and their calves and between the fathers and their children—when neither the calves nor the children needed so much care—He began to wonder why this extraordinary thing had happened. He was astonished to see all the residents of Vrindavana as affectionate to their own children as they had been to Krishna. Balarama concluded that this mystical change must have been caused by Krishna. So Balarama inquired from Krishna about the actual situation. He said:

"My dear Krishna, in the beginning I thought that all these calves and cowherd boys were either great sages and saintly persons or *devatas*, but at present it appears that they are actually Your expansions. They are all You; You Yourself are playing as the calves and boys. What is the answer to this mysterious situation? Where have those original calves and boys gone? Why are You expanding Yourself as the calves and boys?" At the request of Balarama, Krishna briefly explained the whole situation: how the calves and boys were stolen by Brahma and how He was concealing the incident so people would not know that the original calves and boys were missing.

* * *

19. The Prayers of Lord Brahma

While Krishna and Balarama were talking, Brahma returned after a moment's interval, though one moment of Brahma is equal to one year of our Earth time. Brahma came back to see the fun caused by his stealing the boys and calves. But he was also afraid that he was playing with fire. Krishna was his master, and he had played mischief for fun by taking away His calves and boys. He saw that all the boys and calves were playing with Krishna in the same way as when he had come upon them, although he was confident that he had taken them and made them lie down, asleep under the spell of his mystic power. Brahma began to think, "All the boys and calves were taken away by me, and I know they are still sleeping. How is it that a similar batch of boys and calves is playing with Krishna? Is it that they are not influenced by my mystic power? Have they been playing continually for one year with Krishna?" Brahma could not understand who they were and how they were still playing, even though he had put them all to sleep. In order to convince Brahma that all those calves and boys were not the original ones, the calves and boys who were playing with Krishna all transformed into radiant four armed forms of Vishnu (Vishnu being an expansion of Krishna). All the Vishnu forms were of bluish colour and dressed in yellow garments and all of Them had four hands decorated with club, disc, lotus flower and conchshell. On Their heads were glittering golden helmets inlaid with jewels; They were bedecked with pearls and earrings and garlanded with beautiful flowers. On Their chests was the mark of *shrivatsa*, Their arms were decorated with armlets and other jewellery, and Their necks were just like conchshells. Their legs were decorated with bells, Their waists with golden belts, and Their fingers with jewelled rings. Brahma also saw that upon the whole body of each Lord Vishnu, beginning from the lotus feet up to the top of the head, fresh *tulasi* leaves and buds had been thrown. All of Them were looking transcendentally beautiful. Their smiling resembled the moonshine, and Their glancing resembled the early rising of the sun. (Vishnu represents the mode of goodness, Brahma represents the mode of passion, and Lord Shiva represents the mode of ignorance. Therefore as the maintainer of everything in the cosmic manifestation, Vishnu is also the creator and maintainer of Brahma and Lord Shiva).

Brahma also saw that many other Brahmas and Shivas and *devatas* and even insignificant living entities down to the ants and very small straws—movable and immovable living entities—were dancing, surrounding Lord Vishnu. Their dancing was accompanied by various kinds of music, and all of Them were worshiping Lord Vishnu. Brahma realized that everything movable and immovable within the cosmic manifestation is an expansion of the energy of the Supreme Lord, and that he too was also a creation of the material energy, just like a puppet. As a puppet has no independent power to dance, but dances according to the direction of the puppet master, so the *devatas* and living entities are all subordinate to the Supreme Personality of Godhead. The only master is Krishna, and all others are His servants.

Krishna took compassion upon Brahma and He suddenly pulled His curtain of Yogamaya over the scene, hiding His amazing powers, so that Brahma would not become more and more perplexed.

When Krishna hid His mystic potencies, Brahma became relieved and seemed to wake up from an almost dead state. He began to open his eyes with great difficulty. He saw all around him the lovely view of Vrindavana—full with trees—and could appreciate its spiritual nature. In the forest of Vrindavana, even ferocious animals like tigers lived peacefully along with the deer and human beings. He could understand that because of the presence of the Supreme Personality of Godhead, Vrindavana is transcendental to all other places and is free from lust and greed.

Brahma then saw Sri Krishna, the Supreme Personality of Godhead, playing the part of a small cowherd boy just as before. He then noticed that the little child was holding a lump of food in His left hand, searching out His friends and calves, just as He had been doing one year earlier, when he had first played his trick and stolen them all away.

Immediately Brahma descended from his great swan carrier and fell down before the Lord just like a golden stick. The word used among the devotees of Krishna for paying respects like this is *dandavat,* and means literally 'falling down like a stick'.

So Brahma, whose complexion was golden, fell down before the Lord with a straight body just like a stick. All four helmets on the four heads of Brahma touched the lotus feet of Krishna. Brahma began to shed tears of joy, and he washed the lotus feet of Krishna with his tears. Repeatedly he fell and rose as he recalled the wonderful activities of the Lord. Seeing the Lord before him, he began to offer prayers with great respect, humility and attention.

Brahma said, "My dear Lord, You are the only worshipful Supreme Lord, the Personality of Godhead; therefore I am offering my humble obeisances and prayers just to please You. Your bodily features are of the colour of clouds filled with water. You are glittering with a silver electric quality emanating from Your yellow garments. My dear Lord, people may say that I am the master of all Vedic knowledge, and I am supposed to be the creator of this universe, but it has been proved now that I cannot understand You, who are appearing just like a simple, uneducated village boy, carrying Your food in Your hand and searching for Your calves. Your appearance as a cowherd child is for the benefit of the devotees, and although I have committed an offence at Your lotus feet by stealing away Your boys and calves, I can understand that You have bestowed Your mercy upon me."

Lord Brahma had realized his actual position; that although he is the supreme creature within this universe, he had no importance in the presence of Lord Krishna. He continued his heartfelt prayers:

"Therefore, my dear Lord, I pray that I may be so fortunate that in this life or in another life, wherever I may take my birth, I may be counted as one of Your devotees. Wherever I may be, I pray that I may be engaged in Your devotional service."

In this way, Brahma, the master of this universe, after offering humble and respectful obeisances to the Supreme Personality of Godhead, whose body is purely spiritual, and having circled Him three times, was ready to return to his abode, known as Brahmaloka. By His gesture, the Supreme Personality of Godhead gave him permission to return home.

* * *

20. Krishna Finds His Friends

As soon as Brahma left, Lord Sri Krishna returned to the bank of the Yamuna and rejoined His calves and cowherd boyfriends, who were situated just as they had been on the very day they had vanished. Krishna had left His friends on the bank of the Yamuna while they were having lunch, and although He returned exactly one year later, the cowherd boys thought that He had returned within a second. They began to laugh, thinking that Krishna was not willing to leave their lunchtime company:

"Dear friend Krishna, You have come back so quickly! All right, we have not yet begun our lunch, so please come and join us, and let us eat together." Krishna smiled and accepted their invitation, and He began to enjoy the lunchtime company of His friends. While eating, Krishna was thinking, "These boys believe that I have come back within a second, but they do not know that for the last year I have been involved with the mystic activities of Lord Brahma."

After finishing their lunch, Krishna and His friends and calves began to return to their homes. While passing, they enjoyed seeing the dead carcass of Aghasura. When Krishna returned home He was seen by all the inhabitants of Vrindavana. He was wearing a peacock feather in His helmet, which was also decorated with forest flowers, and He was garlanded with flowers and painted with different coloured minerals, red oxides, collected from the caves of Govardhana Hill. Each of them had a bugle made of buffalo horn and a stick and a flute, and each called his respective calves by their particular names. All the *gopis* in Vrindavana saw beautiful Krishna entering the village and everyone was so proud of His wonderful activities that they all sang His glories. The boys composed nice songs describing how they were saved from being swallowed by the great serpent and how the serpent was killed. Some described Krishna as the son of Yashoda and others as the son of Nanda Maharaja. "He is so wonderful that He saved us from the clutches of the great serpent and killed him," they said. But little did they know that one year had passed since the killing of Aghasura.

* * *

21. Playing in the Forests

Given charge of the cows, Krishna and Balarama passed through Vrindavana, purifying the land with Their lotus footprints. Accompanied by the cowherd boys and Balarama, Krishna brought along the cows and played on His flute as He entered the forest, which was full of flowers, vegetables, and pasturing grass. There were chirping birds and clear lakes with waters that could relieve one of all fatigue. Sweet-smelling breezes always blew, refreshing the mind and body. Krishna saw all the trees, overloaded with fruits and fresh twigs, bending down to touch the ground as if welcoming Him. He was pleased by the behaviour of the trees, fruits and flowers, and He began to smile, realizing their desires.

Krishna then spoke affectionately to His elder brother Balarama as follows:

"My dear brother, You are superior to all of us, and Your lotus feet are worshiped by the *devatas*. Just see how these trees, full with fruits and flowers, have bent down to worship Your lotus feet. It appears that they are trying to get out of the darkness that has obliged them to accept the form of trees. Actually, the trees born in the land of Vrindavana are not ordinary living entities. In previous lives they have held the mistaken impersonal point of view, thinking they could merge and become one with God, and so they have been put into this stationary condition of life.

But now they have the opportunity of seeing You in Vrindavana, and they are praying for further advancement in spiritual life through Your personal association. I think the bees that are buzzing all around You must have been Your devotees in their past lives. They cannot leave Your company because no one can be a better, more affectionate master than You, since You are the supreme worshipable Godhead. Just see how the peacocks are dancing before You in great ecstasy. The deer, whose behaviour is just like that of the *gopis*, are welcoming You with the same affection. And the cuckoos who are residing in this forest are also welcoming You with their joyful, sweet cries because they consider that Your appearance in their home is so auspicious. Even though they are trees and animals, these residents of Vrindavana are glorifying You. As for the land, it is so pious and fortunate because the footprints of Your lotus feet are marking its body."

Krishna and Balarama were garlanded with forest flowers. While walking, the cowherd boys sometimes imitated the quacking sound of the swans in the lakes, or when they saw the peacocks dancing, they imitated them. Krishna also moved His neck, imitating the peacock's dancing and making His friends laugh.

The cows Krishna looked after had different names, and He would call them with love. After hearing Krishna calling, the cows would respond by mooing, and the boys would enjoy this exchange to their hearts' content. They would all imitate the sounds of the different birds, especially the *chakoras*, peacocks, and cuckoos. Sometimes, when they saw the weaker animals fleeing out of fear of the sounds of tigers and lions, the boys, along with Krishna and Balarama, would imitate the animals and run away with them. When they felt tired, they sat down, and Balarama would put His head on the lap of one of the boys to take rest, and Krishna would come and begin massaging His legs. Sometimes Krishna would take a palm leaf and fan the body of Balarama, causing a pleasing breeze to relieve Him of His fatigue. Other boys would sometimes dance or sing while Balarama took rest, and sometimes they would wrestle amongst themselves or jump. When Krishna felt tired, He would sometimes take shelter of the root of a big tree or the lap of a cowherd boy, and lie down. When He lay down with a boy or a root as His pillow, some of the boys would come and massage His legs, and some would fan His body. Some of the more talented boys would sing in sweet voices to please Him. Thus very soon His fatigue would go away. The Supreme Personality of Godhead, Krishna, whose legs are tended by the goddess of fortune, shared Himself with the cowherd boys as one of them, expanding His internal potency to appear exactly like a village boy. But despite His appearance, there were occasions when He proved beyond all doubt that He was the Supreme Personality of Godhead. Sometimes ordinary men pose themselves as the Supreme Personality of Godhead and cheat innocent people with some cheap display of magic, but they can only cheat; they cannot exhibit the full potency of God.

* * *

22. The Killing of Dhenakasura

While Krishna was thus engaged in His transcendental pastimes yet another opportunity arose for Him to exhibit His superhuman powers. His most intimate friends Sridhama, Subala and Stoka Krishna had a problem:

"Dear Balarama and Krishna, You are very expert in killing all kinds of disturbing demons. Kindly note that just near this place there is a big forest called Talavana which has many palm trees filled with fruits. Ripened fruit from those trees even litters the ground. It is a lovely place, but because of a great ass demon, Dhenakasura, it is difficult to go there and collect the fruits. Dear Krishna and Balarama, this ass demon is surrounded by similar demon friends who have all assumed the same shape. All of them are extremely strong and only You can kill them. Even other animals like birds and deer have all left there out of fear. Dear Krishna, to tell You frankly, we are greatly attracted by the sweet aroma of this place. If You like, let us all go there and enjoy these fruits."

When Balarama and Krishna heard their friends request, They were inclined to please them, and with smiling faces They all proceeded towards the forest. As soon as they entered the Talavana forest, Balarama began to yank the trees with His arms, exhibiting the strength of an elephant. Because of this jerking, all the ripe fruits fell down on the ground. Upon hearing the sound of the falling fruits, the demon Dhenakasura approached with great speed. His hooves pounded the earth with such force that the trees moved as if there were an earthquake. The demon kicked Balarama's chest with his hind legs. At first Balarama did not react, but with great anger the demon kicked Him again even more violently. This time Balarama caught hold of the legs of the ass with one hand and, wheeling him around, threw him high into the treetops. While he was being wheeled around by Balarama, the demon lost his life. The demon's body was so heavy that the palm tree he landed in fell upon other trees, and several fell down. It appeared as if a great hurricane had passed through the forest as trees fell one after another. This exhibition of strength is not so astonishing since Balarama is actually the Personality of Godhead known as Ananta Sesha Naga, who is holding all the planets on His millions of heads.

After the demon had been thrown into the trees, all the friends and associates of Dhenakasura immediately assembled and attacked Balarama and Krishna with great force. They were determined to retaliate and avenge the death of their friend. But Krishna and Balarama caught each of the asses by the hind legs and, exactly in the same way, wheeled them around. Thus They killed all of them and threw them high into the palm trees, their dead bodies resembling clouds of various colours caught in the treetops. Hearing of this great incident, the *devatas* from the higher planets showered flowers on Krishna and Balarama and beat their drums and offered devotional prayers.

A few days after the killing of Dhenakasura, people

began to come into the Talavana forest to collect the fruits, and animals began to return without fear to feed on the lush grasses growing there.

When Krishna, Balarama and Their friends came back to the village of Vrindavana, They played Their flutes, and the boys praised Their uncommon activities in the forest. All the *gopis* in Vrindavana remained morose when Krishna was absent. All day they were thinking of Krishna in the forest or of Him herding cows in the pasture. When they saw Krishna returning, all their anxieties were immediately relieved, and they began to look at His face the way drones hover over the honey of the lotus flower. When Krishna entered the village, the young gopis smiled and laughed. Krishna, while playing the flute, enjoyed the beautiful smiling faces of the gopis. Then Krishna and Balarama were received by Their affectionate mothers, Yashoda and Rohini. They were bathed and given palatable dishes by Their mothers, and They pleasantly ate everything. After eating, They were seated on clean bedding, and the mothers began to sing various songs of Their activities which made them quickly fall asleep. In this way, Krishna and Balarama used to enjoy Vrindavana life as cowherd boys.

* * *

23. The Kaliya Serpent

Krishna used to go with His boyfriends, and sometimes with Balarama too, to the bank of the Yamuna to tend the cows. Gradually the summer season arrived and one day, while in the field, the boys and cows became thirsty and began to drink the river water. They did not realise, however, that the river had been made poisonous by the venom of the great serpent known as Kaliya. Because the water was so poisonous, the boys and cows became affected immediately after drinking it. They suddenly fell down on the ground, apparently dead. Then Krishna, who is the life of all that lives, simply cast His merciful glance over them, and all the boys and cows regained consciousness and began to look at one another with great astonishment. They could understand that by drinking the water of the Yamuna they had all died and that the merciful glance of Krishna had restored their life. Thus they appreciated the mystic power of Krishna, who is known as Yogeshvara, the master of all mystic yogis.

Within the river Yamuna there was a great lake, and in that lake the black serpent Kaliya lived. Because of his poison, the whole area was so contaminated that it emanated a poisonous vapour twenty-four hours a day. If a bird happened to even pass over the spot, it would immediately die and fall down in the water. Due to the poisonous effect of the serpent, the trees and grass near the bank of the Yamuna had all dried up and died. Lord Krishna saw the effect of the great serpent's poison; the whole river running through Vrindavana was now deadly.

Krishna, who advented Himself just to kill all undesirable elements in the world, quickly climbed up into a big *kadamba* tree on the bank of the Yamuna. (The *kadamba* is a rare tree bearing round, yellow flowers that is generally only found in the Vrindavana area). After climbing to the top of the tree, He tightened His belt cloth and, flapping His arms just like a wrestler, jumped into the midst of the poisonous lake. The *kadamba* tree from which Krishna had jumped was the only tree in the area which had survived the toxic atmosphere. When Lord Krishna jumped into the water the river over-flooded its banks to a distance of one hundred yards, as if something very large had fallen into it.

Krishna swam about just like a strong elephant and made so much noise that the great black serpent Kaliya could easily hear Him. He realised he was under attack and so moved to strike Krishna first. When Kaliya approached Krishna, he saw that His body was beautiful and delicate; its colour resembling that of a cloud, and His legs resembling a lotus flower. He was decorated with jewels and yellow garments. He was smiling with a beautiful face and was playing in the river Yamuna with great strength. But in spite of Krishna's beautiful features, Kaliya felt great anger within his heart, and thus he grabbed Krishna with his mighty coils. Seeing the incredible way in which Krishna was enveloped in the coils of the serpent, the affectionate cowherd boys and other inhabitants of

Vrindavana, who were now watching from the river bank, became stunned out of fear. They had dedicated everything to Krishna and when they saw Him in that condition they became overwhelmed with fear and fell down on the ground. All the cows, bulls and small calves were also overwhelmed with grief, and they began to look at Him with great anxiety.

While all this was taking place on the bank of the Yamuna, there were ill omens manifesting, such as the earth trembling and meteors falling from the sky. Observing the inauspicious signs, the cowherd men, including Maharaja Nanda, became fearful. To make things worse they heard that Krishna had gone to the pasturing ground without His elder brother, Balarama. As soon as Nanda and Yashoda and the cowherd men heard this news, they became even more anxious. Out of their great affection for Krishna, and being unaware of the extent of His potencies, they were overwhelmed with grief and anxiety. They thought, "Today Krishna is surely going to be vanquished!"

All the inhabitants of Vrindavana came out of the village to find Krishna. While this was happening, Balarama, who is the master of all knowledge, stood there simply smiling. He knew how powerful His younger brother Krishna was and that there was no cause for anxiety when He was fighting with an ordinary serpent of the material world. He did not, therefore, personally take any part in their sorrow. The inhabitants of Vrindavana began to search out Krishna by following the impression of His footprints on the ground, and thus they moved hastily towards the bank of the

Yamuna. Finally, by following the footprints, which are marked with flag, bow and conchshell, the inhabitants of Vrindavana arrived at the riverbank. There they found all the cows and boys weeping at the sight of Krishna wrapped in the coils of the fearsome black serpent. Mother Yashoda wanted to enter the river Yamuna, and when she was stopped, she fainted. Her friends, who were equally aggrieved, were shedding tears like torrents of rain, but in order to bring mother Yashoda to consciousness, they began to speak loudly about the transcendental pastimes of Krishna. Mother Yashoda remained still, as if dead, because her consciousness was concentrated on the face of Krishna. Nanda and all the other cowherd men were ready to enter the waters of the Yamuna, but Lord Balarama stopped them because He was in perfect knowledge that there was no real danger.

For two hours Krishna remained like an ordinary child gripped in the coils of Kaliya, as though helpless, but when He saw that all the inhabitants of Gokula were on the point of death through fear, Krishna quickly freed Himself. He began to expand His body, and when the serpent tried to hold Him, he felt a great strain. On account of the strain, his coils slackened, and he had no choice but to free Krishna from his grasp. Kaliya then seethed with even greater anger, and his great hoods expanded. He exhaled poisonous fumes from his nostrils, his eyes blazed like fire, and flames issued from his mouth. The great serpent remained still for some time, looking at Krishna and licking his many lips with forked tongues. Krishna immediately pounced upon him, just as Garuda swoops upon a snake.

Kaliya looked for an opportunity to bite Him, but Krishna moved too swiftly around him. As Krishna and Kaliya moved in a circle, the serpent gradually became fatigued, and his strength faded. Krishna then pressed down the serpent's hoods and jumped up on them. The Lord's lotus feet became tinged with red from the rays of the jewels on the snake's hoods. Then Krishna began to dance upon the hoods of the serpent, although they were moving to and fro. Upon seeing this, the denizens of the upper planets showered flowers, beat drums, played different types of flutes and sang various prayers and songs. In this way, all the denizens of heaven, such as the Gandharvas, Siddhas and *devatas*, became greatly pleased. While Krishna was dancing on his hoods, Kaliya tried to push Him down with some of his other hoods. Kaliya had about a hundred hoods, but Krishna took control of them all. He began to dash Kaliya with His lotus feet, and this was more than the serpent could tolerate. Gradually, Kaliya was reduced to struggling for his very life. He vomited and exhaled fire. While throwing up poisonous material from within, Kaliya's sinful life became purified more and more. Out of great anger he tried to raise one of his hoods to kill the Lord. Krishna captured that hood and subdued it by kicking it and dancing on it. This incredible exhibition of Krishna's strength is to be expected since He is the reservoir of all strength.

It appeared as if Krishna was being worshiped since the floods of poisons emanating from the serpent's mouth resembled flower offerings. Kaliya then began to vomit blood instead of poison; he was now completely worn out.

His whole body appeared to be broken by the kicks of the Lord. Within his mind he finally began to understand that Krishna was the Supreme Personality of Godhead, and he decided he must surrender to Him.

The wives of the serpent, known as the Nagapatnis, saw that their husband had been subdued by the Lord's kicking and that he was almost at the point of death. They also surrendered to the Supreme Lord and began to pray. They appeared before Him, put forward their offspring and anxiously offered respectful obeisances, falling down on the bank of the Yamuna.

"O dear Lord," the Nagapatnis said, "we consider that Your punishment is Your great mercy upon us. When You punish someone it is to be understood that the reactions of his previous sinful activities are destroyed. It is already clear that this creature must have been full of sin; otherwise, how could he have obtained the body of a serpent in the first place. It is therefore most auspicious that You have punished him in this way. You can appreciate that this poor serpent is about to give up his life. You know that for us women our husbands are our life, our everything; therefore, we are praying that You kindly excuse this great offender- Kaliya."

After the Nagapatnis submitted their prayers, Lord Krishna released Kaliya from his punishment. Kaliya was already unconscious from being struck by the Lord. Upon regaining consciousness Kaliya humbly began to pray to the Supreme Lord Krishna with folded hands:

"My dear Lord, I am born as a serpent; therefore, by natural instinct I am very angry and envious. How is it then possible to give up my acquired nature without Your mercy? It is very difficult to get out of the clutches of Your *maya* (illusory energy). My dear Lord, kindly excuse me. I surrender unto You. Now You can punish me or save me, as You desire."

After hearing this, the Supreme Personality of Godhead ordered the serpent thus:

"You must leave this place and go to the ocean. Leave without delay. You can take with you all your offspring, wives and everything that you possess. Do not pollute the waters of the Yamuna ever again. Let it be drunk by My cows and cowherd boys without hindrance." The Lord then declared that the order given to the Kaliya snake be recited and heard by everyone so that no one need fear Kaliya any longer. The Lord also assured Kaliya: "You came here out of fear of Garuda, who wanted to eat you in the beautiful land by the ocean. Now, after seeing the marks where I have touched your head with My lotus feet, Garuda will not disturb you." The Lord was pleased with Kaliya and his wives. Immediately after hearing His order, the snake and his wives began to worship Him with offerings of fine garments, flowers, garlands, jewels, ornaments, sandalwood pulp, lotus flowers and delicious fruits. In this way they pleased the master of Garuda, of whom they were very much afraid. Then, obeying the orders of Lord Krishna, all of them left the lake within the Yamuna.

Anyone who hears with devotion the story of the Kaliya serpent and his punishment will fear no more the envious activities of snakes.

* * *

24. Why Kaliya Came to the Yamuna

The island known as Nagalaya was inhabited by snakes, and Kaliya was one of the chief serpents there. Being accustomed to eating snakes, Garuda (the half man half eagle carrier of Lord Vishnu) used to come to this island and kill many serpents at will. Some of them he actually ate, but some were unnecessarily killed. The reptile society became so disturbed that their leader, Vasuki, appealed to Lord Brahma for protection. Lord Brahma made an arrangement by which Garuda would not create a disturbance: on each half-moon day, the reptile community would offer a serpent to Garuda. The serpent was to be kept underneath a tree as a sacrificial offering. Garuda was satisfied with this offering, and therefore he did not disturb any other serpents. But gradually, Kaliya took advantage of this situation. He was unnecessarily puffed up by the amount of poison he had accumulated, as well as by his strength, and he thought, "Why should Garuda be offered this sacrifice?" He then ceased offering any snakes to Garuda but ate them all himself. When Garuda understood that Kaliya was eating the sacrifices meant for him, he became extremely angry and rushed to the island to kill the offensive serpent. Kaliya tried to fight Garuda and faced him with his many hoods and poisonous sharp teeth. Kaliya attempted to bite him, and Garuda in great anger struck the body of Kaliya with his effulgent golden wings. Kaliya immediately fled to the lake known as Kaliya-hrada, which lay within the

Yamuna River and which Garuda could not approach.

Kaliya took shelter within the water of the Yamuna for the following reason. Just as Garuda went to the island of the Kaliya snake, he also used to go to the Yamuna to catch fish to eat. There was, however, a great yogi known as Saubhari Muni, who used to meditate under the water and who liked the fish that swam there. He asked Garuda not to come to this place any more to disturb the fish. Although Garuda did not have to obey the sage, being the carrier of Lord Vishnu, he nevertheless obeyed the order of the great yogi. Instead of staying and eating many fish, he carried off one big fish, who was their leader. Saubhari Muni was sorry that one of the leaders of the fish was taken away by Garuda, and thinking of their protection, he cursed Garuda with the following words: "Henceforward, from this day, if Garuda comes here to catch fish, then—I say this with all my strength—he will be immediately killed."

This curse was known only to Kaliya. Kaliya was therefore confident that Garuda would not be able to come there, and so he thought it wise to take shelter in that place. It may be noted that Garuda is as powerful as the Supreme Personality of Godhead, being an incarnation of His spiritual energy, and so can never be subject to anyone's order or curse. Actually the cursing of Garuda was an offence on the part of Saubhari Muni. Although Garuda did not try to retaliate due to this offence, Saubhari fell down from his yogic position and afterwards became an ordinary householder in the material world. The fall down of Saubhari Muni is a stern warning to anyone who may think of offending a devotee of Krishna.

* * *

25. The Forest Fire and the Demon Pralambasura

When Krishna finally came out of Kaliya's lake, He was seen by all His friends and relatives on the bank of the Yamuna. He appeared before them nicely decorated, smeared all over with sandalwood paste, bedecked with valuable jewels and stones, and almost completely covered with gold. The inhabitants of Vrindavana saw Krishna coming from the Yamuna, and it was as though they had recovered their very lives. They each in turn pressed Krishna to their chests, feeling great relief. Balarama also embraced Krishna, but He was laughing because when everyone else was so overwhelmed with anxiety, He had known all along that Krishna would be victorious. The *brahmana* inhabitants of Vrindavana came with their wives to congratulate Krishna and His family members. Mother Yashoda simply embraced Krishna and made Him sit on her lap while she shed tears continuously.

Since it was almost night, and all the inhabitants of Vrindavana, including the cows and calves, were very tired, they decided to rest on the riverbank. In the middle of the night, while they were sleeping, a forest fire broke out. It spread so quickly that it seemed as though everyone would be engulfed in its flames. As soon as they felt the warmth of the fire, they rushed to take shelter of Krishna, the Supreme Personality of Godhead. They began to say, "Our dear Krishna! O Supreme Personality of Godhead! Our dear Balarama, the reservoir of all strength! Please try to save us from this all-devouring and devastating fire. We have no shelter other than You. This devastating fire will swallow us all!" Lord Krishna, being compassionate towards the residents of Vrindavana, immediately swallowed up the whole forest fire and saved them. This was not impossible for Krishna because He is unlimited, and so has the power to do anything He desires.

After extinguishing the devastating fire, Lord Krishna, surrounded by His relatives, friends, cows, calves and bulls and glorified by His friends' singing, again entered Vrindavana. While Krishna and Balarama were enjoying life in Vrindavana, the season gradually changed to summer. The summer season in India is not so welcome because of the excessive heat, but in Vrindavana everyone was pleased because there it appeared just like spring. This was possible only because Lord Krishna and Balarama were residing there. In Vrindavana there were many water falls, and the sound was so sweet that it covered the sound of the crickets. And because water flowed all over, the forest always looked green and beautiful.

The inhabitants of Vrindavana were never disturbed by the scorching heat of the sun or the high summer temperatures. The lakes of Vrindavana are surrounded by green grasses, and various kinds of lotus flowers bloom there. When the particles of water from the waves of the Yamuna, the lakes and the waterfalls touched the bodies of the inhabitants of Vrindavana, they felt a cooling effect. Therefore they were undisturbed by the summer season.

Vrindavana is such a lovely place. Flowers are always blooming, and there are even various kinds of decorated deer. Birds are chirping, peacocks are crowing and dancing, and bees are humming. The cuckoos there also sing melodiously in five different tunes.

Krishna, the reservoir of pleasure, blowing His flute, accompanied by His elder brother Balarama and the other cowherd boys and the cows, entered the beautiful forest of Vrindavana to enjoy the atmosphere. They walked into the midst of newly grown leaves of trees whose flowers resembled peacock feathers. They were garlanded by those flowers and decorated with saffron chalk. Sometimes they were dancing and singing and sometimes wrestling with one another. While Krishna danced, some of the cowherd boys sang, and others played on flutes; some bugled on buffalo horns or clapped their hands, praising Krishna, "Dear brother, You are dancing so nicely." Actually, all these boys were *devatas* descended from higher planets to assist Krishna in His pastimes.

Up to that time, neither Balarama nor Krishna had undergone the haircutting ceremony; therefore Their hair was clustered like crows' feathers. They were always playing hide-and-seek with Their boyfriends or jumping or fighting with them. Sometimes, while His friends were chanting and dancing, Krishna would praise them, "My dear friends, you are dancing and singing very nicely." The boys played at catching ball with fruits such as *bael* and *amalaka*. They played blind man's buff, challenging and touching one another. Sometimes they imitated the forest deer and various kinds of birds. They joked with one another by imitating croaking frogs, and they enjoyed swinging underneath the trees. Sometimes they would play like a king and his subjects amongst themselves. In this way, Balarama and Krishna, along with all Their friends, played all kinds of sports and enjoyed the soothing atmosphere of Vrindavana, full of rivers, lakes, fine trees and excellent gardens filled with fruits and flowers.

Once while the boys were playing, a great demon called Pralambasura entered their company, desiring to kidnap both Balarama and Krishna. Although Krishna was playing the part of a cowherd boy, as the Supreme Personality of Godhead He could understand everything—past, present and future. So when Pralambasura approached, Krishna began to think how to kill the demon, though externally He received him as a friend.

"O My dear friend," He said. "It is very good that you have come to take part in our pastimes." Krishna then called all His friends and ordered them: "Now we shall challenge one another in pairs." With this proposal, all the boys assembled together. Some of them took the side of Krishna, and some of them took the side of Balarama, and in this way they arranged themselves into two teams. Whichever team lost the wrestling would have to carry the victorious members on their backs, as a horse carries its master. They began playing and soon Balarama's team, which included Sridhama and Vrishabha, came out victorious, and so Krishna's team had to carry them on their backs through the Bhandiravana forest. Krishna had to carry Sridhama on His back, and Bhadrasena carried Vrishabha. Imitating their play, Pralambasura, who changed his form to look just like an innocent cowherd boy, carried Balarama on his back. Pralambasura had calculated that Krishna was the most powerful of all the cowherd boys and so to avoid Him he carried Balarama far away.

The demon was undoubtedly very strong and powerful, but he was carrying Balarama, who is compared to a mountain. He began to feel Balarama as a heavy burden, and thus he assumed his real form as a massive demon wearing a golden helmet and earrings. Balarama observed the demon's body expanding up to the limits of the clouds, his eyes dazzling like blazing fire and his mouth flashing with sharp teeth. At first, Balarama was surprised by the demon's appearance, and He began to wonder, "How is it that all of a sudden this little boy who was carrying me has changed in every way?" But with a clear mind He could quickly understand that He was being carried away from His friends by a demon who intended to kill Him. Immediately He struck the head of the demon with His strong fist. Being stricken by the fist of Balarama, the demon fell down dead with blood pouring from his mouth, just like a snake with a smashed head. When the demon fell, he made a tremendous sound as though a great hill were collapsing after being struck by the thunderbolt of King Indra. All the boys then rushed to the spot. Astonished by the ghastly scene, they began to praise Balarama with the words,"Well done, well done." All of them embraced Balarama with great affection, as though He had returned from death. All the *devatas* in the heavenly planets became satisfied and showered flowers on the transcendental body of Balarama, and offered their blessings and congratulations for His having killed such a great demon.

The killing of Pralambasura and the devouring of the devastating forest fire by Krishna and Balarama became household topics in Vrindavana. The cowherd men described these wonderful activities to their wives and to everyone else, and all were struck with wonder. They concluded that Krishna and Balarama were *devatas* who had kindly come to Vrindavana as their children.

* * *

26. Autumn Arrives

Eventually the rainy season came. In India, after the scorching heat of the summer, the rainy season is most welcome. The clouds accumulating in the sky, covering the sun and the moon, are pleasing to the people in general as they expect rainfall at every moment. The thunder and occasional lightning are equally pleasurable as they indicate refreshment and new life for all living things.

The Vrindavana forest improved from the rains and became full with ripened dates, mangoes, blackberries and other fruits. Lord Krishna, the Supreme Personality of Godhead, along with His boyfriends and Lord Balarama, entered the forest to enjoy the new seasonal atmosphere. The cows, being fed by fresh grasses, became very healthy, and their milk bags were all full. When Lord Krishna called them by name, they came to Him out of affection, and in their joyful condition the milk flowed from their bags. On the bank of the Yamuna He saw all the trees decorated with beehives pouring honey. There were many waterfalls on Govardhana Hill, and their flowing made a pleasant sound. Krishna and His companions would sit under a tree or within the caves of Govardhana Hill and enjoy eating the ripened fruits and talking with great pleasure. When Krishna and Balarama were in the forest, mother Yashoda used to send Them some fruits, sweetmeats and rice mixed with yogurt. Krishna would take them, sit down on a slab

of stone on the bank of the Yamuna, and call His friends
to join Him. While Krishna and Balarama and Their friends
were eating, they watched the cows, calves and bulls. The
cows appeared to be a little tired from standing with their
heavy milk bags, but when they sat and chewed the grass
they became happy, and Krishna was pleased to see them.
He was proud to see the beauty of the forest due to the
rainy season since He knew it was nothing but the result
of His own energy, acting completely under His direction.

While Krishna and Balarama were enjoying the gifts of
the rainy season in this way, the autumn season gradually
arrived. With the appearance of autumn the sky became
completely cleared of all clouds, and recovered its natural
blue colour. The lotus flowers in the lakes grew in large
numbers because of the absence of lilies. Both the lilies
and the lotus flowers grow in sunshine, but during the
autumn season the scorching sun helps only the lotus.
This is compared to a country where the king or the
government is strong. In such a country the unwanted
elements like thieves and robbers cannot prosper. When
the citizens become confident that they will not be attacked
by robbers, they develop with great satisfaction. A strong
government is compared to the scorching sunshine in the
autumn season, the lilies are compared to unwanted
persons like robbers, and the lotus flowers are compared
to the satisfied citizens. In Vrindavana, at that time, the
autumn season was particularly beautiful because of the
presence of the Supreme Personality of Godhead, Krishna
and Balarama.

* * *

27. The Gopis are attracted by Krishna's Flute

With the arrival of the beautiful autumn season, the lakes and rivers became as clear as crystal and filled with fragrant lotus flowers, while pleasant breezes blew all around. At that time, Krishna entered the forest of Vrindavana with the cows and cowherd boys. Krishna was very pleased with the atmosphere of the forest, where flowers bloomed and bees and drones hummed jubilantly. While the birds, trees and plants were all looking happy, Krishna, tending the cows and accompanied by Sri Balarama and the cowherd boys, began to play His transcendental flute. After hearing the vibration of Krishna's flute, the *gopis* in Vrindavana began to talk amongst themselves about how nicely He was playing. When the *gopis* were describing the sweet vibration of Krishna's flute, they also remembered their pastimes with Him; thus their minds became disturbed. While discussing His flute playing, which made a transcendental sound vibration, they remembered how Krishna dressed, decorated with a peacock feather on His head, just like a dancing actor with blue flowers pushed over His ear. His garment glowed yellow-gold, and He was garlanded with a necklace. Dressed in such an attractive way, Krishna filled up the holes of His flute with the nectar emanating from His lips.

Krishna was expert in playing the flute, and the *gopis*

were captivated by its sound. One of the *gopis* told her friends: "The highest perfection of the eyes is to see Krishna and Balarama entering the forest and playing Their flutes and tending the cows with Their friends." It is confirmed in the *Bhagavad-gita* that anyone who is always absorbed in the thought of Krishna is the topmost of all yogis. Another *gopi* expressed her opinion that Krishna and Balarama, while tending the cows, appeared just like actors going to play on a dramatic stage. Krishna was dressed in glowing garments of yellow, Balarama in blue, and They held new twigs of mango tree, peacock feathers and bunches of flowers in Their hands. Dressed with garlands of lotus flowers, They were sometimes singing very sweetly among Their friends. One *gopi* told her friend: "Why do Krishna and Balarama look so beautiful?"

Another *gopi* said: "My dear friends, we cannot even think of His bamboo flute—what sort of pious activities did it perform so that it is now enjoying the nectar of the lips of Krishna?" The *gopis* asked, "How is it possible that the flute, which is nothing but a bamboo rod, is always engaged in enjoying the nectar from Krishna's lips? Because the flute is engaged in the service of the Supreme Lord, the mother and the father of the flute must be so happy." The lakes and the rivers are considered to be the mothers of the trees because the trees live simply by drinking water. So the waters of the lakes and rivers of Vrindavana were in a happy mood, full of blooming lotus flowers, because the waters were thinking, "How is it that our son, the bamboo rod, is enjoying the nectar of Krishna's lips?" The bamboo trees standing by the banks of the rivers and lakes were also happy to see their descendant so engaged in the service of the Lord. The trees were overwhelmed with joy and were constantly yielding honey, which flowed from the beehives hanging on the branches. In the spiritual world everything is fully conscious, even the trees, plants and rivers. Another *gopi* said: "When Govinda (Krishna) plays His flute, the peacocks immediately become mad, and when the animals, trees and plants, either on the top of Govardhana Hill or in the valley, see the dancing of the peacocks, they all stand still and listen to the transcendental sound of the flute with great attention. We think that this boon is not possible or available on any other planet."

Although the *gopis* were village cowherd women and girls, they had extensive Vedic knowledge. Such is the effect of Vedic civilization. People in general would learn the highest truths of the *Vedas* simply by hearing from authoritative sources. Nowadays people's ideas are formed by television, magazines and atheistic education. That is why there is such a great lack of spiritual knowledge, and hence so many problems in modern society. Another *gopi* declared:

"My dear friends just see the deer! Although they are dumb animals, they have approached the son of Maharaja Nanda, Krishna. Not only are they attracted by the dress of Krishna and Balarama, but as soon as they hear the playing of the flute, the deer, along with their husbands, offer respectful obeisances to the Lord by looking at Him with great affection." The *gopis* were envious of the deer because the deer were able to offer their service to Krishna along with their husbands. The *gopis* thought themselves not so fortunate because whenever they wanted to go to Krishna, their husbands were not at all happy.

Another *gopi* said, "Even the wives of the denizens of heaven become attracted after hearing the transcendental sound of His flute. Although they are travelling in the air in their airplanes, enjoying the company of their husbands, on hearing the sound of Krishna's flute, they immediately become agitated." The transcendental sound of the flute of Krishna travelled to all corners of the universe.

Another *gopi* said to her friends, "My dear friends, the cows are also charmed as soon as they hear the transcendental sound of the flute of Krishna. As for the calves, they are seen with the nipples of their mothers pressed in their mouths, but they cannot suck the milk. They remain struck with devotion, and tears glide down from their eyes, illustrating vividly how they are embracing Krishna heart to heart."

Another young *gopi* told her mother, "My dear mother, the birds, who are all looking at Krishna playing His flute, are sitting attentively on the branches and twigs of different trees. From their features it appears that they have forgotten everything except the sound of Krishna's flute. This proves they are not ordinary birds, but great sages and devotees who have appeared in Vrindavana forest as birds just to hear Krishna play." Even the river Yamuna, desiring to embrace the lotus feet of Krishna after hearing the transcendental vibration of His flute, broke her fierce waves to flow gently with lotus flowers in her hands, just to present them to Krishna with deep feeling.

The scorching heat of the autumn sunshine was sometimes intolerable. On such occasions clouds appeared out of sympathy in the sky above Krishna and Balarama and Their boyfriends while They played Their flutes. The clouds served as a soothing umbrella over Their heads just to make friendship with Krishna. Krishna and Balarama carried binding ropes on Their shoulders and in Their hands, just like ordinary cowherd boys. While milking the cows, the boys bound their hind legs with this rope. In spite of Their being the Supreme Personality of Godhead, They played exactly like cowherd boys, and therefore everything became wonderful and attractive. As for the *gopis*, their only purpose was to remain always absorbed in thoughts of Krishna.

* * *

28. Stealing the Garments
of the Gopis

In Vedic civilization unmarried girls from ten to fourteen years of age are often encouraged to worship Lord Shiva or goddess Durga in order to get a good husband. But the unmarried girls of Vrindavana were already attracted by the beauty of Krishna. Even so they worshipped goddess Durga daily, early in the morning after taking a bath in the river Yamuna. The goddess is worshiped by preparing a doll made of sand from the bank of the Yamuna. It is said in the Vedic scriptures that a deity can be made from different materials: it can be painted, made of metal, jewels, wood, earth or stone or can be conceived within the mind or heart of the worshiper. It is also said that such authorised forms are taken to be non-different from either the Supreme Lord or whichever *devata* is being worshipped.

The unmarried *gopis* used to prepare the deity of goddess Durga and worship it with sandalwood paste, garlands, incense, lamps and all kinds of presentations consisting of fruits, grains and twigs of plants. After worshiping, it is the custom to pray for some blessing. The unmarried girls used to pray with great devotion to goddess Durga (or Katyayani as she is also called), addressing her as follows:

"O supreme external energy of the Personality of Godhead, O supreme mystic power, O supreme controller of this material world, O goddess, please be kind to us and arrange for our marriage with the son of Nanda Maharaja, Krishna."

Devotees of Krishna do not normally worship the *devatas*, since usually such worship is done for material benefits. Yet the *gopis*, who are beyond compare in their affection for Krishna, were seen to worship Durga. The difference here is that the *gopis* were praying to the goddess to become wives of Lord Krishna which was a purely spiritual desire. Their goal was Krishna, not something ordinary, and they worshiped goddess Durga for a whole month to achieve their purpose. Early in the morning, after the *gopis* had bathed in the Yamuna, they would all hold hands and loudly sing of the wonderful pastimes of Krishna. It is an old system among Indian girls and women that when they take a bath in the river they place their garments on the bank and dip into the water. No men were allowed in the portion of the river where the girls and women bathed, as is still the system today. The Supreme Personality of Godhead, knowing the minds of the unmarried young *gopis*, granted their desire. At the end of the month, Krishna, who was now seven or eight years old, along with His friends, came to where they were bathing and quickly collected all the garments of the *gopis*. Krishna then climbed up into a nearby tree, and with a smiling face began to speak to them:

"My dear girls," He said, "please come here one after another and pray to Me for your garments and then take them away. I have no desire to play any joke with you; I know you are tired from worshiping goddess Durga for the last one month. Please do not come here all at the same time. Come alone; one at a time, since I want to see each of you."

When the girls in the water heard such joking words from Krishna, they began to look at one another and smile. They were joyous to hear such a request from Krishna because they were already in love with Him. Out of shyness they looked at one another, but they could not come out of the water. They had been in the water so long they shivered with cold, yet upon hearing the pleasing, joking words of Govinda (Krishna), their minds were joyful. They told Krishna:

"Dear son of Nanda Maharaja, please do not joke with us in that way. It is completely unfair. You are the respectable son of Nanda Maharaja, and You are most dear to all of us, but You should not play this joke because now we are all shivering from the cold water. Kindly deliver our garments this minute; otherwise we shall suffer." They then began to appeal to Krishna with humble words: "We are all Your eternal servants. Whatever You order us to do; we are obliged to perform without hesitation because we consider it our religious duty. But if You insist on putting this proposal to us, which is impossible to perform, then certainly we will have to go to your father, Nanda Maharaja, and make a complaint against You. If Nanda Maharaja does not take action, then we shall tell King Kamsa about Your misbehaviour." Upon hearing this appeal by the unmarried *gopis*, Krishna answered:

"My dear girls, if you think that you are My eternal servants and you are always ready to execute My order, then My request is that, with your smiling faces, you please come up here alone, one at a time, and take back your garments. If you do not come here, however, and if you complain about me to My father, I shall not care since I know My father is too old to take any action against Me."

When the *gopis* saw that Krishna was strong and determined, they had no alternative but to do as he asked. One after another they came out of the water, shivering, and covering themselves with their hands. Their simple behaviour was so pure that Lord Krishna immediately became pleased with them. All the unmarried *gopis* who prayed to Durga to have Krishna as their husband were thus satisfied and they became the greatest lovers of Krishna, and His most obedient servants.

"My dear *gopis*," Krishna continued, "your desire to have Me as your husband will be fulfilled. I promise that during the next autumn season you shall be able to meet with Me."

Later on Krishna, in the company of His cowherd boyfriends, took shelter of the shade of some trees and became very happy.

"My dear friends," Krishna said, "just look at these most fortunate trees of Vrindavana. They have dedicated their lives to the welfare of others. Individually they are tolerating all kinds of natural disturbances, such as hurricanes, torrents of rain, scorching heat and piercing cold, but still they are careful to relieve our fatigue and give us shelter. They supply all sorts of benefits to human society, such as leaves, flowers, fruit, shade, roots, bark, flavour extracts and fuel for cooking. They sacrifice everything for the

welfare of all living entities like noble men who give charity to all who approach them."

Thus the Supreme Personality of Godhead walked on the bank of the Yamuna, touching the leaves of the trees and their fruits, flowers and twigs, and praising their glorious welfare activities. After seeing the young *gopis* bathing in the Yamuna, Krishna passed the rest of the morning with the boys.

* * *

29. Delivering the Wives
of the Brahmanas

The morning had passed and the cowherd boys were very hungry since they had not had breakfast. They approached Krishna and Balarama saying:

"Dear Krishna and Balarama, we are so hungry. Please arrange for something to take away our hunger."

Requested in this way by Their friends, Lord Krishna said:

"My dear friends please go to the house of the *brahmanas* who live nearby to ask for something to eat. They are now performing Vedic sacrifices in the hope of attaining the heavenly planets. All of you please go to them." Then Lord Krishna warned His friends, "These *brahmanas* are not our devotees. They cannot even chant Our names, 'Krishna' and 'Balarama'. They are busy chanting Vedic hymns, forgetting that the purpose of all Vedic knowledge is to find Me."

Charity is generally given to high-class *brahmanas*, but Krishna and Balarama did not appear in a *brahmana* family. Balarama was known as the son of Vasudeva, a *kshatriya* (the kingly class), and Krishna was known in Vrindavana as the son of Nanda Maharaja, who was a *vaishya* or a member of the merchant class. Neither belonged to the *brahmana* community. Therefore, Krishna considered that the *brahmanas* who were performing Vedic sacrifices might not want to give charity to a *kshatriya* and *vaishya* who they would see as inferior to themselves.

"But at least if you utter the name of Balarama, they are more likely to give in charity to a *kshatriya* than to Me, because I am only a *vaishya*." Krishna advised.

Being thus ordered by the Supreme Personality of Godhead, all the boys went to the *brahmanas* and began to ask for some charity. They approached them with folded hands and fell down on the ground to offer respect:

"O earthly gods, we were ordered to come to you by Lord Krishna and Balarama who are tending cows nearby, and who we have accompanied. We have come to ask for some food from you since You are all *brahmanas* and have knowledge of religious principles. Please give us some food so we can eat it with Krishna and Balarama."

But the *brahmanas*, who were simply obsessed with rituals and complicated sacrifices, could not understand that the request of these devotees of the Lord was actually transcendental. They refused to even speak to the boys. Despite their great learning and impressive knowledge of Vedic sacrificial rites, all such *brahmanas*, although they think of themselves as highly elevated, are in fact ignorant of the real purpose of sacrifice. They do not know the purpose of the Vedas, as it is explained in the *Bhagavad-gita:* to understand, serve and love Krishna.

When the boys saw that the *brahmanas* would not reply to them even with a simple yes or no, they became very disappointed. They returned to Lord Krishna and Balarama and explained what had happened. After hearing this, the Supreme Personality of Godhead smiled. He told them that they should not be sorry or disappointed because that is the way of begging, you cannot always be successful. Lord Krishna then asked all the boys to go again, but this time to approach only the wives of those *brahmanas*. He also informed them that these wives were great devotees.

"They are always absorbed in thinking of Us. Go there and ask for some food in My name and the name of Balarama, and I am sure that they will give you as much as you desire," Krishna said.

Carrying out Krishna's order, the boys went to the wives of the *brahmanas* who they found sitting inside a house, beautifully decorated with ornaments. After offering them all respects, the boys said:

"Dear mothers, Lord Krishna and Balarama are nearby with the cows, and They asked us to come and see you here. All of us are extremely hungry; therefore we have come to you for some food."

Upon hearing this request, the wives of the *brahmanas* became anxious for Krishna and Balarama. They did not have to be convinced, but straight away, upon hearing the names of Krishna and Balarama, they became most eager to see Them. By thinking of Krishna constantly, these wives of the *brahmanas* were performing the greatest form of mystic meditation. All the wives then busily filled different pots with delicious food that had been carefully prepared for the sacrifice. After collecting a feast, they all got ready to go and see their beloved Krishna.

For a long time the wives had been eager to see Krishna. However, when they were preparing to leave, their husbands, fathers, sons and relatives asked them not to go. But the wives did not listen. When a devotee is called by the attraction of Krishna, he does not care for bodily ties. The women entered the forest of Vrindavana on the bank of the Yamuna, which was lush with vegetation and newly grown vines and flowers. Within that forest they saw Krishna and Balarama tending the cows along with Their affectionate boyfriends.

The *brahmanas*' wives saw Krishna with a blackish complexion, wearing a garment that glittered like gold. He wore a pleasing garland of forest flowers and a peacock feather on His head. He was also painted with the minerals found in Vrindavana, and He looked exactly like a dancing actor on a theatrical stage. They saw Him keeping one hand on the shoulder of His friend, and in His other hand He was holding a lotus flower. His ears were decorated with lilies, He wore *tilaka*, and He was smiling charmingly. With their very eyes the wives of the *brahmanas* saw the Supreme Personality of Godhead, of whom they had heard so much, who was so dear to them, and in whom their minds were always absorbed. Now they saw Him eye to eye and face to face, and Krishna entered within their hearts through their eyes.

Within themselves they began to embrace Krishna to their hearts' content and they no longer felt the distress of separation. As the Supersoul living in everyone's heart, Lord Krishna could understand their minds; that they had come to Him despite all the protests of their relatives and despite all the duties of their household life. He therefore began to speak to them, smiling magnificently.

"My dear wives of the *brahmanas*," Krishna said,

sweetly, "you are all very fortunate and welcome here. I know in order to come here you have had to overcome so many restrictions placed on you by your families. Having seen Me you can now return to your homes. Engage yourselves in the service of your husbands so that they will be pleased with you, and so the sacrifice which they have begun can be properly executed."

The wives of the *brahmanas* replied: "Dear Lord, this sort of instruction does not befit You. Your eternal promise is that You will always protect Your devotees, and now You must fulfil this vow. We have surrendered to Your lotus feet, which are covered by *tulasi* leaves, so we have no desire to return to the company of our so-called relatives, who in any case will not take us back since we left them without permission. We have no shelter to return to. Please, therefore, arrange for us to live eternally under Your protection."

"My dear wives of the *brahmanas*," The Supreme Personality of Godhead replied, "rest assured that your husbands will not neglect you on your return, nor will your brothers, sons, or fathers refuse to accept you. Because you are My pure devotees everyone will be satisfied with you."

Krishna is situated as the Supersoul in everyone's heart, so if someone becomes a pure devotee of Lord Krishna, he immediately becomes pleasing to everyone. After being instructed by Krishna, all the wives returned home to their respective husbands. Pleased to see their wives return, the *brahmanas* sat together with them and carried out their sacrifices. But the *brahmanas* began to regret their sinful act of refusing food to the Supreme Personality of Godhead. They could finally understand their mistake; that in spite of being engaged in performing so-called Vedic rituals, they had neglected the Supreme Personality of Godhead Himself, who had appeared just like an ordinary human being asking for some food. They began to condemn themselves after seeing the faith and devotion of their wives.

"To hell with our being born *brahmanas!* To hell with our learning all the Vedic scriptures! To hell with our performing great sacrifices and observing all the rules and regulations! To hell with our family! To hell with our expert service in performing the rituals exactly according to the description of the scriptures! To hell with it all, for we have not developed transcendental loving service to the Supreme Personality of Godhead, who is beyond the speculation of the mind, body and senses."

It was proper that the learned *brahmanas* were regretful. If one does not develop Krishna consciousness, then all other religious duties are simply a waste of time and energy. Women in general, being more simple at heart, can easily take to Krishna consciousness, develop love of Krishna and thus get liberation from the clutches of *maya* (material illusion). The *brahmanas* continued, "These women have developed transcendental love for Krishna, the Lord of all mystic yogis! They have surpassed all of us in firm faith and devotion to Krishna. Being too attached to a materialistic way of life, despite our high birth and learning, we did not actually understand the real goal. Even though we were reminded of Krishna and Balarama by the cowherd boys, we ignored Them. We therefore pray to the Lord to be kind enough to excuse us for being under His illusory energy (*maya*). We disobeyed His order without knowing His transcendental glories."

The *brahmanas* wanted to go personally to offer their obeisances to Krishna, but being afraid of Kamsa, they did not do so. Their wives, on the other hand, were so inspired by pure devotional service that they were not in the least afraid. They immediately went to Krishna without thinking of their own safety or bodily comfort.

After the departure of the *brahmanas'* wives, Krishna and His cowherd boyfriends enjoyed the food they had been given. In this way the ever-joyful Personality of Godhead exhibited His transcendental pastimes in the guise of an ordinary human being in order to attract the common people to Krishna consciousness.

* * *

30. Worshiping Govardhana Hill

After this episode with the *brahmanas,* Krishna and Balarama saw that the cowherd men in Their own community were preparing a similar sacrifice in order to satisfy Indra, the King of heaven, who is responsible for supplying rain. A pure devotee is not required to worship any *devatas*, since being a devotee of Lord Krishna, and serving Him with love and devotion, is perfection enough. Krishna wanted to firmly establish pure devotional service exclusively to Himself. So Krishna asked Nanda Maharaja:

"My dear father, what is this arrangement going on for a great sacrifice? What is the result of such a sacrifice, and for whom is it meant? How is it performed? Will you kindly let Me know?" Nanda Maharaja remained silent, thinking that the *yajna* (sacrifice) would be too complicated for his young boy to understand. But Krishna persisted: "Nothing should be kept secret from family members and friends, therefore please let Me know the purpose of the sacrifice you are going to perform." Maharaja Nanda replied:

"My dear boy, this ceremony is more or less traditional. Because rainfall is due to the mercy of King Indra, and because water is so important for our living, we must show him some gratitude. King Indra has kindly sent us clouds to pour down a sufficient quantity of rain for our farming activities, therefore we must satisfy him with this sacrifice."

After hearing this, Krishna spoke in such a way as to make King Indra extremely angry.

Krishna suggested that they cancel the sacrifice. He gave two main reasons for doing this. First, as stated in the *Bhagavad-gita,* there is no need to worship the *devatas* for any material advancement; all results derived from worshiping the *devatas* are simply temporary, and only those who are less intelligent are interested in temporary results. Secondly, Krishna argued that whatever temporary result one derives from worshiping the *devatas* is actually granted by the Supreme Personality of Godhead, who is in charge of all the *devatas.* In order to stop the worship of Indra, Krishna cleverly began to talk as if He were an atheist supporting the philosophy of *karma-mimamsa.* People who teach this philosophy question the need to worship and accept the supreme authority of God.

"My dear father," Krishna said, "I don't think you need to worship any *devata* for success in farming. Every living being is born according to his past karma (action and reaction) and leaves this life simply taking the result of his present karma. Everyone is born in different species of life according to his past activities, and he gets his next birth according to the activities of this life. Different grades of material happiness and distress, comforts and disadvantages of life, are simply the direct results of activities performed either in a past or present life."

Nanda Maharaja replied that without satisfying the *devatas*, and instead just performing some material activity, they would not get any good result. But Lord Krishna defeated this argument saying:

"There is no need to worship the *devata* Indra. Everyone has to achieve the result of his own work. The *devatas* will be satisfied if we just perform all our duties, so there is no need to worship them. The proper duty of the *brahmanas* is the study of the Vedas; the proper duty of the royal order, the *kshatriyas*, is engagement in protecting the citizens; the proper duty of the *vaishya* community is agriculture, trade and protection of the cows; and the proper duty of the *shudra* is service to the higher classes, namely the *brahmanas, kshatriyas* and *vaishyas*. We belong to the *vaishya* community, and our proper duty is to farm, to trade with the agricultural produce, to protect cows or to take to banking. Even if you do not please Indra, what can he do? He pours water on the ocean also, where there is no need of water, and where he is never worshipped. Since he pours water on the ocean then how can rain depend on him being worshipped? In this village our specific relationship is with Govardhana Hill and Vrindavana forest; nothing more. I therefore request you, My dear father, to begin a sacrifice which will satisfy the local *brahmanas* and Govardhana Hill, and let us have nothing to do with Indra."

After hearing this statement by Krishna, Nanda Maharaja replied: "My dear boy, since You are asking, I shall arrange for a separate sacrifice for the local *brahmanas* and Govardhana Hill. But for the present let me execute this sacrifice known as Indra-yajna."

"My dear father," Krishna replied, "don't delay. The sacrifice you propose for Govardhana Hill and the local *brahmanas* will take much time. Better take everything you have already collected together for the Indra-yajna and immediately use it to satisfy Govardhana Hill and the local *brahmanas* instead."

Unable to defeat Krishna's arguments Maharaja Nanda finally relented. The cowherd men then inquired from Krishna how He wanted the *yajna* performed, and Krishna gave them the following directions:

"Prepare very nice foods of all descriptions from the grains and *ghee* collected for the yajna. Prepare rice, *dhal*, then *halava, pakora, puri* and all kinds of milk preparations, such as sweet rice, sweetballs, *sandesha, rasagulla* and *laddu*, and invite the learned *brahmanas* who can chant the Vedic hymns and offer oblations to the fire. The *brahmanas* should be given all kinds of grains in charity. Then decorate all the cows and feed them well. After performing this, give money in charity to the *brahmanas*. As far as the lower animals are concerned, such as the dogs, and the lower grades of people, they also may be given sumptuous *prasadam* (food offered to the Lord). After lush grasses have been given to the cows, the sacrifice known as Govardhana-puja may immediately begin. This sacrifice will greatly satisfy Me."

From that day onwards Govardhana-puja has been going on and is also known as Annakuta. In all the temples of Vrindavana and elsewhere, huge quantities of sumptuous food are prepared in this ceremony and then distributed to the general population.

The Supreme Personality of Godhead, Krishna, advised the cowherd men to stop the Indra-yajna and begin the Govardhana-puja in order to chastise Indra, who was overly puffed up at being the controller of the heavenly planets.

The honest and simple cowherd men, headed by Nanda Maharaja, accepted Krishna's proposal and executed in detail everything He advised. They performed Govardhana worship and then walked around the hill, just as residents of Vrindavana do to this very day.

When everything was complete, Krishna assumed a great transcendental form and declared to the inhabitants of Vrindavana that He Himself was non-different from Govardhana Hill. Then Krishna began to eat all the food offered there. The identity of Krishna as Govardhana Hill is still honoured, and great devotees take rocks from Govardhana Hill and worship them exactly as they worship the Deity of Krishna in the temples. Krishna Himself, along with the other inhabitants of Vrindavana, offered obeisances to the Deity as well as Govardhana Hill. Krishna then declared:

"In order to assure the good fortune of the cows and themselves, all people of Vrindavana near Govardhana must worship the hill, as prescribed by Me. One who neglects the worship of Govardhana-puja, as I am personally conducting it, will not be happy. There are many snakes on Govardhana Hill, and persons neglecting Govardhana-puja will be bitten by them and killed."

After performing the Govardhana-puja sacrifice as instructed by Krishna, all the inhabitants of Vrindavana returned to their respective homes.

* * *

31. Devastating Rainfall
in Vrindavana

When Indra understood that his sacrifice had been stopped by Krishna, he became angry. As the director of different kinds of clouds, Indra called for the Samvartaka. This cloud is used to devastate the whole universe and it was ordered by Indra to go over Vrindavana and inundate the whole area with an extensive flood. Indra was puffed up by his material position, and he wanted to challenge the supreme controller thinking himself, at least at that point, to be as powerful as Krishna. Indra said:

"Just see the impudence of the inhabitants of Vrindavana! They are simply forest dwellers, but being infatuated with their friend Krishna, who is nothing but an ordinary human being, they have dared to defy the *devatas*."

Krishna has declared in the *Bhagavad-gita* that worshipers of the *devatas* are not very intelligent. He has also stated that one should give up all other kinds of worship and simply concentrate on Krishna.

"These cowherd men in Vrindavana have neglected my authority on the advice of this talkative boy known as Krishna," Indra continued, "because they have taken Krishna so seriously, they must be punished. They should be destroyed along with all their cows." When King Indra ordered the Samvartaka and other clouds to destroy Vrindavana in this way, they became fearful of doing such mischief. But King Indra assured them, "You go ahead, and I will also go with you, riding on my elephant, accompanied by great storms. And I shall apply all my strength to punish the inhabitants of Vrindavana."

Being ordered by King Indra, all the dark, dangerous clouds appeared above Vrindavana and began to pour water incessantly, with all their strength and power. There was constant lightning and thunder, blowing of severe wind and incessant falling of rain, which felt like piercing sharp arrows. By pouring water as thick as pillars, without cessation, the clouds gradually filled all the lands in Vrindavana with water, and there was no visible distinction between higher and lower land. The situation was extremely dangerous, especially for the animals. The rainfall was accompanied by great winds, and every living creature in Vrindavana began to tremble from the severe cold. Unable to find any other source of help, they all approached Krishna and began to pray:

"Dear Krishna, You are all-powerful, and You are very affectionate to Your devotees. Now please protect us, who have been attacked by angry Indra."

Krishna then considered Indra's actions, "This *devata* who thinks himself supreme has shown his great power, but I shall answer him according to My position, and I shall teach him that he is not in charge of managing the universe. I am the Supreme Lord over all, and I shall therefore take away his false pride. I shall give protection to My pure devotees in Vrindavana, who are at present completely at My mercy and whom I have taken completely under My protection. I must save them by My mystic power."

Thinking in this way, Lord Krishna picked up

Govardhana Hill with one hand, exactly as a child picks up a mushroom from the ground, and held it aloft on just His little finger. Lord Krishna then addressed His devotees, "My dear brothers, My dear father, dear inhabitants of Vrindavana, you can now safely enter under the umbrella of Govardhana Hill, which I have just lifted. Do not be afraid of the hill and think that it will fall from My hand. Be happy along with your animals under this shelter." Being assured by Lord Krishna, all the inhabitants of Vrindavana entered safely beneath the great hill, along with their property and animals, where they remained for one week without being disturbed by hunger, thirst or any other discomfort. They were simply astonished to see how Krishna was holding up the mountain with the little finger of His left hand.

Seeing the extraordinary mystic power of Krishna, Indra, the King of heaven, was completely baffled. He immediately called for all the clouds and asked them to stop. The sky became completely cleared of all clouds, the sun rose and the strong wind stopped. At that time Krishna said:

"My dear cowherd men, now you can leave and take your wives, children, cows and valuables because the flooding has stopped along with the swelling waters of the river."

All the men loaded their valuables on carts and slowly left with their cows and other belongings. After they had cleared out everything, Lord Krishna very slowly replaced Govardhana Hill exactly in the same position it had been before. When everything was done, all the inhabitants of Vrindavana approached Krishna with feelings of love and embraced Him with great ecstasy.

* * *

32. Prayers by Indra, the King of Heaven

When Krishna saved the inhabitants of Vrindavana from the wrath of Indra by lifting Govardhana Hill, a *surabhi* cow from Goloka Vrindavana (the spiritual world), as well as King Indra from the heavenly planets, appeared before Him. Indra realised he had made a serious offence to Krishna; therefore he cautiously came to Him in a secluded place and fell down at His lotus feet. Indra knew that Krishna was his master, but he could not believe that Krishna could come down and live in Vrindavana just like an ordinary child. When Krishna defied the authority of Indra, he had become angry because he thought that no one was as powerful as he. But after this incident his false pride was destroyed. Being conscious of his inferior position, he appeared before Krishna with folded hands and began to offer the following prayers:

"My dear Lord," Indra said, "being puffed up by my false prestige, I thought that You had offended me by not allowing the cowherd men to perform the Indra-yajna, and I thought that You wanted to enjoy the offerings that were arranged for the sacrifice; but I mistook Your position. Now by Your grace I can understand that You are the Supreme Lord, the Personality of Godhead, and the original father of this cosmic manifestation. My dear Lord, I committed a great offence to You; therefore please kindly excuse me. Kindly give me Your blessings so that I may not act so foolishly again. I take shelter of Your lotus feet."

Thus praised by Indra, Lord Krishna, the Supreme Personality of Godhead, smiled beautifully and then replied in a grave voice like a rumbling cloud: "My dear Indra, I stopped your sacrifice just to show you My causeless mercy and to remind you that I am your eternal master. I am not only your master, but of all the other *devatas* as well. I can show anyone My favour, and I can chastise anyone, because no one is superior to Me. If I find someone overcome by false pride, in order to show him My causeless mercy I withdraw all his opulences."

It is noteworthy that Krishna sometimes removes all of a rich man's opulences in order to help that individual soul to surrender to Him. Krishna can remove the wealth, strength, fame, intelligence or beauty of anyone, since He is the original source of all those qualities. When Krishna appears in this world He shows that there is no-one superior to Himself, not even powerful *devatas* such as Brahma and Shiva.

After instructing Indra, Lord Krishna asked him to return to his kingdom in the heavenly planets and to always remember that he is never the supreme but always subordinate to Himself, the Supreme Personality of Godhead. He also advised him to remain as King of heaven but to be careful of false pride.

After this the transcendental *surabhi* cow, who had come with Indra to see Krishna, offered her respectful obeisances and worshiped Him. Then the *surabhi* cow bathed Krishna with her milk, and Indra and all the *devatas* bathed Him with water from the celestial Ganges. Lord Krishna was pleased with all of them. King Indra then took His permission to return to his heavenly kingdom.

* * *

33. Releasing Nanda Maharaja from the clutches of Varuna

On the eleventh day of the full moon, known as Ekadashi, Maharaja Nanda observed fasting for the whole day, and the next morning, known as Dwadashi, he went to take a bath in the river Yamuna. He entered deep into the water of the river, but was arrested immediately by one of the servants of Varunadeva (the *devata* of the oceans), who brought Nanda Maharaja before his master, accusing him of bathing at the wrong time. According to astronomical calculations, the time in which he took bath was considered demoniac. When Nanda Maharaja disappeared into the river his companions began to call loudly for Krishna and Balarama who straight away understood what had happened. Being committed to protecting the inhabitants of Vrindavana. They also went to the abode of Varuna. The *devata* Varuna received Lord Krishna and Balarama with great respect and said:

"My dear Lord, actually at this very moment, because of Your presence, my life as the *devata* Varuna has become successful. Just by seeing You I shall never again have to accept another material body. Therefore, O Lord, let me offer my respectful obeisances to You. I am very sorry that my foolish servant has mistakenly arrested Your father. Please forgive me; You can take him back immediately."

In this way Lord Krishna, the Supreme Personality of Godhead, rescued His father and presented him before his friends, bringing them great happiness. Nanda Maharaja was surprised that although the *devata* Varuna was so opulent, he offered such enormous respect to his own little son Krishna. That was quite astonishing to Nanda, and he began to describe the incident to his friends and relatives with great wonder.

Actually, although Krishna was acting so wonderfully, Maharaja Nanda and mother Yashoda could not think of Him as the Supreme Personality of Godhead. Instead, they always accepted Him as their beloved child. Krishna led all the cowherd men, headed by Nanda Maharaja, to a lake where they took their bath. It was then that Krishna revealed to them the real nature of the Vaikunthalokas (the spiritual planets in the spiritual world). After seeing the spiritual sky and the Vaikunthalokas, all the men felt wonderfully blissful, and upon coming out of the lake, they saw Krishna, who was being worshiped with excellent prayers.

Within the material world, every conditioned soul is in the darkness of ignorance, thinking that this material world is everything, and that his material body is his true self. Because they have very little information of the spiritual world, the mass of people do not generally take to spiritual activity, which is called *bhakti-yoga*. Those who successfully practice *bhakti-yoga* go directly to the spiritual world after giving up their present body. Therefore it is recommended that one should take to *bhakti-yoga* and keep himself engaged twenty-four hours a day in Krishna consciousness, which places one beyond the reach of the modes of material nature (goodness, passion and ignorance). One in Krishna consciousness can easily understand his own identity as a pure spirit soul, and also the nature of the spiritual sky.

* * *

34. The Gopis Meet Krishna in the Forest

At the very moment Krishna desired to enjoy the company of the *gopis* in the forest, the moon suddenly appeared in the sky displaying its most beautiful features. It was the full moon of the *sharat* season, and with its rising the whole sky appeared smeared by red *kunkuma*, increasing Krishna's desire to dance with the *gopis*. The forests were filled with fragrant flowers and the atmosphere was cooling and festive. When Lord Krishna began to blow His flute, the *gopis* all over Vrindavana became enchanted. Their attraction to the vibration of the flute increased a thousand times due to the rising full moon, the red horizon, the calm and cool atmosphere and the blossoming flowers. All these *gopis* were by nature very attracted to Krishna's beauty, and when they heard the vibration of His flute, they strongly desired to satisfy Krishna's senses.

Upon hearing the vibration of the flute, the *gopis* left what they were doing and ran swiftly to the spot where Krishna was standing, their earrings swinging back and forth. Some of them were breast-feeding their small babies, and some were engaged in distributing food to the members of their families, but they left all such engagements and immediately rushed towards the spot where Krishna was playing His flute. Some were serving their husbands, and some were themselves eating, but caring neither to serve their husbands nor eat, they left. Some of them had been decorating their faces with cosmetic ointments and trying to dress themselves agreeably before going to Krishna, but unfortunately they only half finished because of their anxiety to meet Krishna. Their faces were decorated hurriedly and haphazardly; some even put the lower part of their clothes on the upper part of their bodies and the upper on the lower.

While all the *gopis* were hurriedly leaving their homes, their relatives could only wonder where they were going. Being young girls, they were supposed to be protected either by husbands, elder brothers or fathers. All their guardians forbade them to go to Krishna, but they disregarded them. When a person becomes attracted by Krishna and is in full Krishna consciousness, he does not care for any worldly duties, even though they may seem urgent. Some of the *gopis* were stopped from going to Krishna by their husbands who locked them in their rooms, and so instead they began to meditate upon His transcendental form by closing their eyes.

When the *gopis* had all assembled, Krishna began to speak as follows:

"O ladies of Vrindavana, you are most fortunate, and you are all so dear to Me. I am very pleased that you have come here, and I hope everything is well in Vrindavana. Now please order Me. What can I do for you? What is the purpose of your coming here in the dead of night? Kindly take your seats and let Me know what I can do for you."

The *gopis* had come to Krishna to enjoy His company, to dance with Him, and when Krishna began to receive them officially, showing all kinds of etiquette, they were surprised. He was treating them as ordinary society women. Therefore they began to smile among themselves, and though they eagerly listened to Krishna, they were surprised at the way He spoke. Then Krishna began to instruct them:

"My dear friends, you must know that it is now the dead of night, and the forest is dangerous. At this time all the ferocious jungle animals—the tigers, bears, jackals and wolves—are prowling in the forest. Everywhere you go you will find that such animals are loitering to find their prey. I think, therefore, that you are taking a great risk in coming here. Please go back without delay."

When He saw that they continued to smile, He said, "I greatly appreciate your beauty. All of you have attractive, thin waists. However, it does not look good for young girls and boys to remain together in the dead of night." After hearing this advice, the *gopis* did not seem at all happy; therefore Krishna began to stress the point in a different way. "My dear friends, I can understand that you have left your homes without the permission of your guardians; therefore I think your mothers, your fathers, your elder brothers and even your sons, not to speak of your husbands, must be anxious to find you. So don't delay. Please go back home and make them peaceful." Becoming somewhat disturbed and angry at Krishna's advice, the *gopis* diverted their attention towards the beauty of the forest which was illuminated by the bright shining of the moon. Krishna took this opportunity to further advise them. "I think you have come out to see the beautiful Vrindavana forest on this night," He said, "but you must now be satisfied. So return to your homes without delay. I understand that you have great affection for Me, and out of that transcendental affection you have come here, hearing My playing on the flute. But for a chaste woman, service to the husband is the best religious principle. It is better for you to go home and just talk about Me and think of Me, and by this process of constantly remembering Me and chanting My names you will surely rise to the spiritual platform. There is no need to stand near Me. Please go back home."

When Krishna spoke in such a discouraging way to the *gopis* they became sad and full of anxiety. They were worried that they would not be able to enjoy the rasa dance with Him. The *gopis* began to breathe heavily and instead of looking at Krishna face to face, they bowed their heads and looked at the ground, drawing curved lines on the ground with their toes. They were shedding heavy tears, and their cosmetic decorations started to run down their faces. The water from their eyes mixed with the *kunkuma* on their breasts and fell to the ground. They could not say anything to Krishna but simply stood there silently. Finally they managed to speak.

"Krishna," they said, "You are most cruel! You should not talk like that. We are fully surrendered souls. Please accept us. Of course, You are the Supreme Personality of Godhead, and You can do whatever You like, but it is not worthy of Your position to treat us in such a way. We have come to You, leaving everything behind, just to take shelter of Your lotus feet. We are Your devotees. Your instructions to women to be faithful to their husbands are surely correct, but we know that all such duties can be perfectly observed by staying under the protection of Your lotus feet. You are the dear-most personality in this world. If a woman accepts You as the supreme husband, then she will never be without a husband. Your beauty is so sublime that not only women, but also men, cows, birds, beasts and even trees, fruits and flowers—everyone and everything—become helplessly attracted."

Upon hearing the anxious plea of the *gopis*, the Supreme Personality of Godhead smiled kindly. When Krishna, smiling, looked at the faces of the *gopis*, the beauty of their faces became a hundred times enhanced. When He was enjoying them in their midst, He appeared just like the full moon surrounded by millions of shining stars. Thus the Supreme Personality of Godhead, surrounded by hundreds of *gopis* and decorated with a flower garland of many colours, began to wander within the Vrindavana forest, sometimes singing to Himself and sometimes singing with the *gopis*. In this way the Lord and the *gopis* reached the cool, sandy bank of the Yamuna, where there were lilies and lotus flowers. In such a transcendental atmosphere, the *gopis* and Krishna began to enjoy themselves. Walking on the bank of the Yamuna, the *gopis* enjoyed Krishna's company without a tinge of mundane lust.

However, the *gopis* soon began to feel proud, thinking themselves to be the most fortunate women in the universe due to being favoured by the company of Krishna. Lord Krishna could understand their pride, and in order to cure them of it He instantly disappeared from the scene. The Supreme Personality of Godhead has six kinds of opulences, and this is an example of His opulence of renunciation.

* * *

35. Krishna's Hiding from the Gopis

When Krishna suddenly disappeared from the company of the *gopis*, they searched for Him everywhere. When they could not find Him anywhere, they became afraid and almost mad after Him. They were simply thinking of the pastimes of Krishna in great love and affection. Being absorbed in thoughts of Him, they experienced loss of memory, and with dampened eyes they saw their own pastimes with Krishna, His beautiful talks with them and other activities. Being so attracted to Krishna, they imitated His dancing, His walking and His smiling, as if they themselves were Krishna. Due to Krishna's absence, they all became crazy; each one of them told the others that she was Krishna Himself. Soon they all assembled together and chanted Krishna's name loudly as they moved from one part of the forest to another, searching for Him.

Actually, Krishna is everywhere; He is in the sky, the forest and within the heart of every living thing. The *gopis* therefore began to question the trees and plants about Krishna. There were various types of big trees and small plants in the forest, and the *gopis* starting talking to them:

"Dear banyan tree, have you seen the son of Maharaja Nanda passing this way, laughing and playing on His flute? He has stolen our hearts and gone away. If you have seen Him, kindly inform us which way He has gone. He has disappeared because of our pride."

The *gopis* knew deep down why Krishna had suddenly disappeared. They knew that although Krishna accepts everyone's service, He does not like it when one devotee proudly considers himself better than others. If sometimes there are such feelings, Krishna ends them by changing His attitude toward the devotee.

After searching for Krishna here and there, the *gopis* became fatigued, and then they began to talk like mad women. They could only satisfy themselves by imitating the different pastimes of Krishna. One of them imitated the demon Putana, while another pretended to be baby Krishna. One *gopi* imitated a hand-driven cart, and another *gopi* lay down beneath the cart and threw up her legs, touching the wheels of the cart. They imitated child Krishna lying down on the ground, and one *gopi* became the demon Trinavarta and carried Krishna by force into the sky; and one of the *gopis* began to imitate Krishna while He was attempting to walk, ringing His ankle bells. One of the *gopis* took another *gopi* on her shoulders, just as Krishna used to take His boyfriends. Absorbed in thoughts of Krishna, the *gopi* who was carrying her friend began to boast that she was Krishna herself:

"All of you just see my movement!" One of the *gopis* raised her hand with her covering garments and said, "Now don't be afraid of the torrents of rain and severe hurricanes. I'll save you!" In this way she imitated the lifting of Govardhana Hill. One *gopi* forcibly put her feet on the head of another *gopi* and said:

"You rascal Kaliya! I shall punish you severely. You must leave this place. I have descended on this earth to punish all kinds of miscreants!" Another *gopi* told her friends:

"Just see! The flames of the forest fire are coming to devour us. Please close your eyes and I shall save you from this imminent danger."

In this way all the *gopis* were madly feeling the absence of Krishna. In some places they found the imprints of the marks on the soles of His feet—namely the flag, the lotus flower, the trident, the thunderbolt, etc. They began to follow the footprints, and shortly they saw another set of footprints beside them, and they realised they were the footprints of Radharani. One *gopi* observed:

"Oh, She is so dear to Him! Krishna must have picked some flowers in this spot to satisfy Radharani, because here, where He stretched on tip toes to get the flowers from the high branches of the tree, we find only half the impression of His feet. Dear friends, just see how Krishna must have sat down here with Radharani and tried to set flowers in Her hair."

All the *gopis* then went further and further into the forest, searching out Krishna, but when they learned that Krishna had also left Radharani alone, they became very sorry. The *gopis* found Radharani all alone, and heard everything from Her— how She misbehaved with Krishna by acting proudly and how She was then insulted for Her pride. After hearing all this, the *gopis* became sympathetic to Her, even though they had previously been feeling somewhat jealous that Krishna had left them for someone else. When they saw it was getting darker, all the *gopis* returned to the bank of the Yamuna and started chanting the glories of Sri Krishna—

Hare Krishna, Hare Krishna, Krishna Krishna, Hare Hare
Hare Rama, Hare Rama, Rama Rama, Hare Hare.

Just by chanting this mantra without offense, anyone can come to know Krishna as perfectly as the *gopis*.

* * *

36. Krishna Returns to the Gopis

When Lord Krishna finally reappeared among the assembled *gopis,* He took them all by the hand on the bank of the Yamuna. It is said in the *Skanda Purana* that out of many thousands of *gopis,* 16,000 are predominant, out of those 16,000, 108 are especially prominent, out of these 108 *gopis,* eight *gopis* are still more prominent, out of those eight *gopis,* Radharani and Chandravali are even more prominent, and out of these two *gopis,* Radharani is the most prominent.

In their previous births, during Lord Ramachandra's appearance, the *gopis* had been Vedic scholars who desired the association of Lord Ramachandra in conjugal love. Ramachandra had given them the benediction that they would be present for the advent of Lord Krishna and He would fulfil their desires. During Krishna's advent, the Vedic scholars took birth as the *gopis* in Vrindavana and they got the association of Krishna in fulfilment of their previous birth's desire. Krishna sat on a seat the *gopis* had made for him and expanded Himself into many Krishnas, so He could appear to be alone with each one of them. Krishna was sitting by the side of each *gopi,* unseen by the others. Having gotten their most beloved Lord, the *gopis* began to please Him by moving their eyebrows and smiling and also by suppressing their anger. Some of them took His lotus feet in their laps and massaged them.

"My dear friends," Krishna said to the *gopis,* "you might be upset by My words and acts, but you must know that sometimes I do not always properly respond to a devotee's feelings for Me. This is to increase their love for Me more and more. If I can be approached by them too easily, they might think, 'Krishna is so easily available.' My dear friends, you have forsaken all kinds of social and religious obligations to come to Me, and I am so obliged to you that I cannot treat you as ordinary devotees. When I left you all alone before I was simply seeing how anxious you were for Me in My absence. So please do not try to find fault with Me." In this way Krishna satisfied the minds of the *gopis* with His sweet words.

* * *

37. Description of the Rasa Dance

From the Vedic literature it appears that when a theatrical actor dances among many dancing girls, it is called a *rasa* dance. When Krishna saw the full-moon night of the *sharat* season, decorated with various seasonal flowers—especially the *mallika* flowers, which are very fragrant—He remembered the *gopis'* prayers to goddess Katyayani (Durga) for Him to be their husband. He then thought this would be a suitable night for a nice dance, and in this way he could fulfil their desire. It appears that Krishna enjoyed the *rasa* dance with the *gopis* when He was eight years old. At that time, many of the *gopis* were married, because in India, especially in those days, girls were married at an early age. At the same time they still hoped Krishna would be their husband. Actually, Krishna is the husband of everyone because He is the supreme enjoyer. We are all female in relation to Krishna who is the supreme male. The *gopis* wanted Krishna to be their husband, even though this was not practically possible. Their tendency to want Krishna as their supreme husband is called *parakiya-rasa*. This type of relationship is ever-present in the spiritual world and cannot be compared in any way to the mundane relationships between men and women in the material world. This material world is nothing but a perverted reflection of the spiritual world. It is stated in *Srimad-Bhagavatam* that one should not imitate this

parakiya-rasa even in a dream or in the imagination. Those who do so drink the most deadly poison since they take Krishna's purely transcendental activities to be on the same level as their own mundane lust.

When Krishna had spoken to pacify the *gopis* they became greatly pleased and were relieved from the suffering of separation. After this, Krishna began His *rasa* dance. The fortunate *gopis* of Vrindavana, who were so attracted to Him, then danced with Krishna, hand in hand.

Krishna's *rasa* dance should never be compared to any kind of mundane dance, such as we find in present day society. The *rasa* dance is completely spiritual. In order to establish this fact, Krishna, the supreme mystic, expanded Himself into many forms and stood beside each *gopi*. Placing His hands on the shoulders of the *gopis* on both sides of Him, He began to dance in their midst. The many mystic expansions of Krishna were not seen by the *gopis;* each *gopi* thought that Krishna was dancing with her alone. Above that wonderful dance flew many airplanes carrying the denizens of the heavenly planets, who were eager to see the spectacle as they showered flower petals. As the *gopis* and Krishna danced together, a blissful, musical sound was produced from the tinkling of their bells, ornaments and bangles. Krishna resembled a greenish sapphire locket in the midst of a golden necklace decorated with valuable stones.

The necks of the *gopis* became tinted with red due to their desire to enjoy Krishna more and more. To satisfy them, Krishna began to clap His hands in time with their singing. The *gopis* wanted to please Krishna, and therefore as Krishna sang; they responded and encouraged Him by saying, "Well done, well done." Sometimes they presented beautiful music for His pleasure, and He responded by praising their singing. When some of the *gopis* became tired from dancing, they placed their hands on Sri Krishna's shoulders. Then their hair loosened and flowers fell to the ground and they became overwhelmed by the fragrance of Krishna's body, which emanated the scent of the lotus, other aromatic flowers and the pulp of sandalwood. The *gopis* so enjoyed the company of Krishna, the husband of the goddess of fortune, that they forgot they had any other husbands in the world, and upon being embraced by the arms of Krishna and dancing and singing with Him, they forgot everything. Touching their bodies with His hands and looking at their pleasing eyes, Krishna enjoyed the *gopis* exactly as a child enjoys playing with the reflection of his body in a mirror. When Krishna touched them, the *gopis* felt surcharged with spiritual energy.

The *gopis* had prayed to the goddess Katyayani to have Krishna as their husband. Now Krishna was fulfilling their desire by expanding Himself in as many forms as there were *gopis*.

People in general should follow the instructions of Lord Krishna as given in the *Bhagavad-gita* and should not even imagine imitating His activities in the *rasa* dance.

* * *

38. Vidyadhara Liberated

Once, the cowherd men of Vrindavana, headed by Nanda Maharaja, desired to go to Ambikavana to observe the Shiva-ratri ceremony. Occasionally devotees of Krishna observe this ceremony because they accept Lord Shiva as the greatest devotee of Krishna. The cowherd men devotedly began to worship the deity of Lord Shiva and Ambika. It is the general practice that wherever there is a temple of Lord Shiva, there must be another temple, of Ambika (or Durga), because Ambika is the wife of Lord Shiva and is the most exalted of chaste women. After reaching Ambikavana, the cowherd men of Vrindavana bathed themselves in the river Saraswati. They then gave the local *brahmanas* cows decorated with golden ornaments and beautiful garlands.

The *brahmanas* are given charity because they are not engaged in any business profession, but only brahminical occupations, as are described in the *Bhagavad-gita*. They must be highly learned and perform austerity and penances. Not only must they themselves be learned, but they must also teach others to become qualified *brahmanas*. If the *brahmanas* receive excess charity, they are to distribute it for the service of Vishnu (Krishna). In the Vedic scriptures, therefore, one is recommended to give charity only to the *brahmanas*, and by so doing one pleases Lord Vishnu and all the *devatas*. There is no such recommendation to give charity directly to unqualified, lazy beggars, since this activity benefits neither the giver nor the receiver.

The cowherd men, headed by Nanda Maharaja, spent that night on the bank of the Saraswati. They fasted all day and drank a little water at night. But while they were taking rest, a great serpent from the nearby forest appeared before them and hungrily began to swallow Nanda Maharaja. Nanda cried out helplessly:

"My dear son, Krishna, please come and save me!" When Nanda Maharaja cried for help, all the cowherd men got up and saw what was happening. They immediately took up burning logs and began to beat the snake to kill it. But in spite of being beaten with burning logs, the serpent carried on swallowing Nanda Maharaja.

At that time Krishna appeared on the scene and touched the serpent with His lotus feet, causing the serpent to shed its reptilian body and appear as a beautiful *devata* named Vidyadhara. He offered obeisances to Lord Krishna and stood before Him with great humility. Krishna then asked the *devata*, "You appear to be a most pleasant *devata*; how is it you performed such abominable activities that you obtained the body of a serpent?" The *devata* then began to narrate the story of his previous life.

"My dear Lord," he said, "in my previous life I was named Vidyadhara and was known all over the world for my beauty. Because I was a celebrated personality, I used to travel everywhere in my airplane. While travelling, I saw a great sage named Angira. He was quite ugly, and because I was so proud of my beauty, I laughed at him. Due to this sinful action, I was condemned by the great sage to assume the form of a serpent."

It is a mistake to think that after reaching the human form of life one can never be degraded to lower species such as the snake. To lose the human form and descend back into the animal species is a huge tragedy, and is considered the greatest type of fear. Animals are always in terror of their lives from other animals who may eat them, and have no idea how to escape their suffering. That is why in the human form it is advised that we take fully to Krishna consciousness so this risk will never arise.

"Now I consider that this curse by the sage was really a great blessing for me." Vidyadhara continued. "Had he not cursed me, I would not have been kicked by Your lotus feet and thus become freed from all material contamination." From this incident we learn that those who are too proud of their material assets, or who are inimical toward others, are degraded to the bodies of snakes. A snake is considered to be the most cruel and envious living entity, but human beings who are envious of others are considered even more vicious than snakes. "My dear Lord," Vidyadhara continued, "now, since I think I have been freed of all kinds of sinful reactions to my past activities, I ask Your permission to return to my abode in the heavenly planets." After receiving this permission, he circled the Lord and offered his respectful obeisances to Him, and then returned home. Thus Nanda Maharaja was saved.

The cowherd men finished their worship and prepared to return to Vrindavana. On the way back they recalled the wonderful activities of Krishna and in that way became more attached to Him. Even though they had initially come to worship Lord Shiva and Ambika, the end result was that they became still more attached to Krishna. If one worships *devatas* like Lord Shiva and Lord Brahma to become more attached to Krishna, then that is approved. But if one goes to the *devatas* for some personal benefit, then that is condemned.

* * *

39. The Slaying of Shankachuda

One pleasant night Krishna and His elder brother Balarama went into the forest of Vrindavana. Accompanied by the damsels of Vrajabhumi (*gopis*), They began to enjoy their company. At that time a demoniac associate of Kuvera (the treasurer of the heavenly planets) appeared on the scene. The demon's name was Shankachuda, because on his head there was a valuable jewel resembling a conchshell. Just as the two sons of Kuvera had been cursed to become trees due to their false pride, this friend of Kuvera was similarly proud. He thought that Krishna and Balarama were two ordinary cowherd boys enjoying the company of many beautiful girls. Generally, in the material world, a person with riches thinks that all beautiful women should be enjoyed by him. Shankachuda thought that since he was so rich it should be he, not Krishna and Balarama, who should enjoy the company of so many beautiful girls, and so he decided to take charge of them. He began to lead the girls away to the north, commanding them as if he were their husband, despite the presence of Krishna and Balarama. Being forcibly taken away by Shankachuda, the damsels of Vraja called out the names of Krishna and Balarama for protection. The two brothers began to follow them, picking up big logs in Their hands.

"Don't be afraid, don't be afraid," They called to the *gopis*. "We are coming to chastise this demon."

Thinking the brothers too powerful, Shankacuda left the *gopis* and ran in fear of his life. But Krishna would not let him go and so, after entrusting the *gopis* to the care of Balarama, He followed Shankachuda, desiring to take the valuable jewel from his head. After following him for a short distance, Krishna caught him, struck his head with His fist and killed him. He then returned with the jewel and, in the presence of all the damsels of Vraja, He presented it as a gift to His elder brother, Balarama.

* * *

40. The Gopis' Feelings of Separation

The *gopis* of Vrindavana were so attached to Krishna that they were not satisfied simply with the *rasa* dance at night. They wanted to associate with Him and enjoy His company during the daytime too. When Krishna went to the forest with His cowherd boyfriends and cows, the *gopis* did not physically take part, but their hearts went with Him. And because their hearts went, they were able to enjoy His company through strong feelings of separation. To acquire this strong feeling of separation from Krishna was the main teaching of Lord Chaitanya, the most recent incarnation of the Lord who appeared five hundred years ago in West Bengal. He taught that the *gopis'* feelings of loving separation from Krishna represented the highest platform of love for God. When we are not in physical contact with Krishna, we can associate with Him like the *gopis*, through feelings of separation. The *gopis* always used to discuss Krishna amongst themselves:

"My dear friends," one *gopi* said, "do you know that when Krishna lies on the ground He rests on His left elbow, and His head rests on His left hand? He also moves His attractive eyebrows while playing His flute with His delicate fingers." Another *gopi* said: "My dear friends, Krishna is so beautiful that the goddess of fortune always remains on His chest, and He is always adorned with a golden necklace. Beautiful Krishna plays His flute in order to enliven the hearts of many devotees. He is the only friend of the suffering living entities." Another *gopi* said: "My dear friends, When He plays on His flute and calls the cows with Balarama, the river Yamuna stops flowing and waits for the air to carry dust from His lotus feet. The river simply remains stunned, stopping its waves, just as we also stop crying for Krishna in expectation."

In the absence of Krishna, the *gopis* were constantly shedding tears, but sometimes, when they thought He was coming, they would stop crying. When they again found he was not coming they cried once more. One *gopi* said: "My dear friends, Krishna and Balarama are nicely dressed with earrings and pearl necklaces. They enjoy Themselves on the top of Govardhana Hill, and when Krishna plays on His flute, the clouds stop their loud thundering out of fear of Him. Rather than disturb the vibration of His flute, they respond with mild thunder to congratulate Krishna, their friend." Another *gopi* told mother Yashoda: "My dear mother, your son is most expert among the cowherd boys. He knows all the different arts of how to tend the cows and how to play the flute. He composes His own songs, and to play them He puts His flute to His mouth. When He plays, either in the morning or in the evening, all the *devatas* listen with great attention. Although they are very learned and expert, they cannot understand the musical arrangements of Krishna's flute and so just become bewildered."

Krishna had many thousands of cows, and they were divided into groups according to their colours. They were also all given different names according to colour. When He was preparing to return from the pasturing ground, He would gather all the cows. As devotees of Krishna count 108 beads when they chant the Hare Krishna *mahamantra* (which represent 108 individual *gopis*), so Krishna would also count on 108 beads to count the different groups of cows.

Everyone has a tendency to love someone. The central point of Krishna consciousness is that Krishna should be the object of our love. By constantly chanting the Hare Krishna mantra and remembering the transcendental pastimes of Krishna, one can stay in full Krishna consciousness and thus make his life sublime and fruitful.

* * *

41. The Aristasura Demon

Once a demon named Aristasura approached the village of Vrindavana in the form of a great bull with a gigantic body and huge horns, digging up the earth with his hooves as he went. When the demon entered Vrindavana, the whole land appeared to tremble, as if there were an earthquake. He roared so fiercely as he entered the village that some of the pregnant cows and women had miscarriages. His body was so big, stout and strong that a cloud hovered over it just as if he were a mountain. All the inhabitants of Vrindavana began to cry, "Krishna! Krishna, please save us!"

Krishna immediately replied:

"Don't be afraid. Don't be afraid." He then appeared before Aristasura and said, "You lowest of creatures! Why are you frightening the inhabitants of Gokula? If you have come to challenge My authority, then I am prepared to fight you."

The demon became extremely angry at Krishna's words and so he furiously ran towards Him with sharp horns, digging up the earth with his hooves and lifting his tail which seemed to be surrounded by clouds. His eyes were reddish and moving in anger. Krishna quickly caught his horns and tossed him away. Although the demon was perspiring and appeared tired, he took courage, got up, and again charged at Krishna with great force and anger.

While rushing towards Krishna, he breathed very heavily. Krishna again caught his horns and threw him to the ground, breaking his horns. Krishna then began to kick his body, and as He did so Aristasura rolled over and kicked his legs violently. Bleeding from the mouth and passing stool and urine, his eyes bulging from their sockets, he rolled over and died. The *devatas* in the celestial planets again showed their appreciation by showering flowers on Krishna. With Balarama, He triumphantly entered Vrindavana village, and the inhabitants glorified Krishna and Balarama with great joy.

* * *

42. Kamsa Sends for Akrura

"You are to be killed by the eighth son of Vasudeva," Narada Muni told Kamsa in his great palace. "That eighth son is Krishna. You were misled by Vasudeva into believing that their eighth baby was a daughter. Actually, the daughter was born of Yashoda, the wife of Nanda Maharaja, and Vasudeva exchanged his son for the daughter in the middle of the night. You were misled. Krishna is the son of Vasudeva, as is Balarama. Being afraid of your atrocious nature, Vasudeva has carefully hidden Them in Vrindavana, out of your sight. Krishna and Balarama have been living secretly in the care of Nanda Maharaja."

Kamsa sat stunned on his throne as he heard Narada speak. He was totally dismayed at this new revelation:

"But I have sent so many demons to kill all the children, how could they possibly have survived?" Kamsa asked.

"All the *asuras* (demons) you sent were themselves killed by Krishna and Balarama. Have you not noticed that none of them ever returned?"

"Vasudeva has tricked me, for this he shall die this very day!" yelled Kamsa as he took out his sword.

"Vasudeva is not the person who will kill you," Narada said, "so what is the point in killing him? Your energy would be better directed in trying to kill Krishna and Balarama."

With that Narada Muni left, singing the name of

Narayana, knowing that he had stirred the situation up so effectively that Kamsa's downfall would come soon.

In a fit of rage Kamsa arrested Vasudeva and his wife, Devaki, and once more had them shackled in iron chains. Acting on the new information, Kamsa called for the deadly Keshi demon and asked him to go to Vrindavana to kill Balarama and Krishna. Then Kamsa called for his expert elephant trainers, as well as his strongest wrestlers including Chanura, Mushtika, Shala and Toshala telling them:

"My dear friends, at Nanda Maharaja's house in Vrindavana there are two brothers, Krishna and Balarama. They are actually two sons of Vasudeva. As you know, I am supposedly destined to be killed by Krishna; there is a prophecy to this effect. Now I am requesting you to arrange for a wrestling match. People from different parts of the country will come to see the festival. I will arrange to get those two boys here, and you will try to kill Them in the wrestling arena." He told the elephant trainers, "Be sure to bring the elephant named Kuvalyapida and keep him at the gate of the wrestling camp. Try to capture Krishna and Balarama on Their arrival and have the elephant kill Them."

Kamsa also advised his friends to arrange worship of Lord Shiva by offering animal sacrifices, along with other ceremonies for his victory. He then called for Akrura, one of the descendants of the Yadus (Krishna's dynasty). When he arrived, Kamsa politely shook his hand.

"My dear Akrura," Kamsa said warmly, trying to conceal his anger," actually I have no better friend than you, so as a friend I am begging charity from you. I request you to go straight away to Vrindavana and find the two boys named Krishna and Balarama. They are sons of Nanda Maharaja. Take this splendid chariot, especially prepared for the boys, and bring Them here as quickly as possible. I tell you frankly my plan is to kill them both. As soon as They come in the gate, there will be a giant elephant named Kuvalyapida waiting to crush Them. But if somehow or other They escape the elephant, They will next meet my most powerful wrestlers and will be killed by them. And after killing these two boys, I shall kill Vasudeva and Nanda, who are supporters of my enemies. I shall also kill my father, Ugrasena, and his brother Devaka, because they are also my enemies. Jarasandha is my loyal father-in-law, and I have a great monkey friend named Dvivida. With their help it will be easy to kill all the kings on the surface of the earth who support Krishna and the *devatas*. This is my plan. In this way I shall be free from all opposition, and I can happily rule the world. So please encourage the boys to come here to see the beauty of Mathura, and take pleasure in the wrestling competition."

After hearing Kamsa's wicked plans, Akrura replied with the following veiled warning:

"My dear King, your plan is excellent. But you should remain steady, because the result may or may not be to your liking. After all, man proposes, God disposes. We may make great plans, but unless they are sanctioned by the supreme authority, they will fail. However, as a friend I shall carry out your order and bring Krishna and Balarama here, as you desire."

* * *

43. Killing the Keshi Demon and Vyomasura

After being instructed by Kamsa, the demon Keshi assumed the form of a terrible horse. He entered the area of Vrindavana with the speed of the mind, his great mane flying, his hooves digging up the earth and neighing loudly. Krishna saw that the demon was terrifying all the residents of Vrindavana with his whinnying and his tail wheeling in the sky like a big cloud. He could understand that the horse was challenging Him to fight. The Lord accepted his challenge and stood before the Keshi demon, calling him on. The horse then ran toward Krishna, making a horrible sound like a roaring lion, his jaws spread wide open as if to swallow the whole sky. Keshi rushed toward the Lord with great speed and tried to trample Him with his legs, which were strong, forceful and as hard as stone. Krishna, however, caught hold of his legs and thus baffled him. Being somewhat angry, Krishna began to whirl the horse around in the air with great ease. After a few rounds, He contemptuously threw him a hundred yards away, just as Garuda throws a big snake. Having been forcefully thrown by Krishna, the horse passed out; but after a little while he regained consciousness and with great anger and force again rushed toward Krishna with his mouth open. As soon as Keshi reached Him, Krishna pushed His left arm straight into the horse's mouth. Krishna's arm felt like a hot iron rod inside the mouth of the horse, who felt great pain as all his teeth suddenly fell out. Krishna began to expand His arm within the mouth of the horse, so choking him. As the great horse suffocated, perspiration appeared on his body, and he threw his legs hither and thither. As his last breath came, his eyeballs bulged in their sockets and he passed stool and urine simultaneously. Thus the vital force of his life expired. When the horse died, his mouth became loose, and Krishna could extract His hand without difficulty. The *devatas* in the sky were amazed, and out of great appreciation they offered Krishna greetings by showering flowers.

After this incident, Narada Muni, the greatest of all devotees, came to see Krishna in a solitary place and began to glorify Him.

"My dear Lord Krishna," he said, "You are the unlimited Supersoul who resides in the hearts of all living beings. You are the witness of all the activities of the living entities, and You are Lord of the whole universe, the master of all the devotees and the Lord of everyone. I am therefore sure that the day after tomorrow I shall see you kill all the demons, and that I shall later see You marry many princesses, the daughters of chivalrous kings." After offering his respectful obeisances to Lord Krishna, Narada Muni took permission and left.

Later that morning, Krishna went to play with His cowherd boyfriends on the top of Govardhana Hill. They were imitating the play of thieves and police while some pretended to be lambs. While they were enjoying themselves, a demon called Vyomasura appeared on the scene. He was the son of another great demon, named Maya, and like many such demons, was able to perform wonderful magic. Vyomasura took the part of a cowherd boy playing as a thief and stole many boys who were playing the parts of lambs. One after another he took away almost all the boys and put them into mountain caves, sealing the entrances with heavy stones. Krishna could understand the trick the demon was playing and caught hold of him exactly as a lion catches a lamb. The demon tried to expand himself like a hill to escape, but Krishna did not allow him to get out of His clutches. Krishna threw the demon on the ground with such great force that he died instantly. After killing the Vyoma demon, Lord Krishna released all His friends from the caves of the mountain. He was then praised by His friends and by the *devatas* for these wonderful acts. He again returned to Vrindavana with His cows and friends.

* * *

44. Akrura's Arrival in Vrindavana

After receiving instruction from Kamsa, Akrura started the next morning for Vrindavana in the fabulous chariot Kamsa had built to tempt Krishna and Balarama to the wrestling match in Mathura. Because Akrura himself was a great devotee of the Lord, while going to Vrindavana he began to pray whilst thinking of Lord Krishna's lotus eyes. A pure devotee always thinks himself unfit to serve Krishna. So Akrura began to think that he was unfit to see the Supreme Personality of Godhead in person. But then Akrura began to think, "By the grace of Krishna everything is possible, and thus if He likes, I will be able to see Him. Just as a blade of grass floating on the waves of a river may by chance come near the shore and gain shelter, a conditioned soul carried away by the waves of material existence may sometimes be saved by the grace of Krishna."

Akrura considered how important Krishna's pastimes were since the people in general could remain constantly in Krishna consciousness just by discussing the Lord's transcendental form, qualities and pastimes. By doing so, the whole universe could actually live peacefully. But without Krishna consciousness, civilization is like a decorated dead body. A dead body may be decorated very nicely, but without consciousness such decorations are useless. Human society without Krishna consciousness is as useless and lifeless as such a dead body. Akrura was also nervous since he had been sent by Krishna's enemy, Kamsa, as part of an evil plan. At the same time, he thought, "Even though I am on a sinful mission, being sent by Kamsa, when I approach the Supreme Personality of Godhead, I shall stand before Him with all humility and folded hands. Surely He will be pleased with my devotional attitude, and maybe He will smile lovingly and look upon me and thereby free me from all kinds of sinful reactions. Unless one is recognized by the Supreme Personality of Godhead, his life cannot be successful."

In this way Akrura meditated on Sri Krishna on his journey from Mathura, reaching Vrindavana by the end of the day when the sun was setting. As soon as he entered the boundary of Vrindavana, he saw the hoof prints of the cows alongside Lord Krishna's footprints, impressed with the signs on the soles of His feet—namely the flag, trident, thunderbolt and lotus flower. Upon seeing the footprints of Krishna, Akrura immediately jumped down from the chariot out of respect. He became overwhelmed with all the symptoms of ecstasy; he wept, his body trembled and he fell flat on his face and began to roll on the ground.

One who intends to visit Vrindavana should follow the ideal footsteps of Akrura and always think of the pastimes and activities of the Lord. As soon as one reaches the boundary of Vrindavana, he should immediately smear the dust of Vrindavana over his body without thinking of his material position and prestige. When Akrura entered Vrindavana, he saw Krishna and Balarama supervising the milking of the cows. Krishna was dressed in yellow garments and Balarama in bluish ones. Akrura also saw that Their eyes were exactly like the beautiful lotus flower that grows during the autumn season. He saw Krishna and Balarama in the spring of Their youth. Although They had the same bodily features, Krishna was blackish in complexion, whereas Balarama was whitish. They had well-constructed bodies, beautiful hands and pleasing faces, and They were as strong as elephants. Without hesitating, Akrura got down from his chariot and fell flat, just like a rod, before Krishna and Balarama. Upon touching the lotus feet of the Supreme Personality of Godhead, he became overwhelmed with transcendental bliss; his voice choked up, and he could not speak. Due to his transcendental pleasure, incessant torrents of tears fell from his eyes. He remained stunned in ecstasy, as if devoid of all powers to see and speak.

Lord Krishna raised Akrura with His hand and embraced him. Balarama also embraced Akrura. Taking him by the hand, Krishna and Balarama brought him to Their home where They offered him a comfortable sitting place and water for washing his feet. They also worshiped him with a special preparation of honey mixed with other ingredients. When Akrura was thus comfortably seated, Krishna and Balarama offered Him a cow in charity and then brought very palatable dishes which Akrura accepted. When Akrura finished eating, Balarama gave him betel nut and spices, as well as pulp of sandalwood, just to make him more pleased and comfortable.

Lord Krishna set the perfect example of how to receive a guest at home. It is a Vedic rule that even if a guest is an enemy he should be received so well that he does not sense any danger from the host. If the host is a poor man, he should at least offer a straw mat as a sitting place and a glass of water to drink. After Akrura was seated, Nanda Maharaja, the foster father of Krishna, said, "My dear Akrura, I know that you are being protected by Kamsa, who is most cruel and demoniac. His protection is just like the slaughterhouse keeper's protection of animals he will kill in the future. Kamsa is so selfish that he has killed the sons of his own sister, so how can I honestly believe that he is protecting the citizens of Mathura?" This statement is just as relevant today, since if the political or executive heads of the state are simply interested in themselves, how can they look after the welfare of the citizens. As Nanda Maharaja spoke to Akrura with pleasing words, Akrura forgot all the fatigue of his day's journey. Akrura was offered a resting place for the night at Nanda Maharaja's house and the two brothers Balarama and Krishna went to take Their supper. Akrura sat on his bed and began to reflect that all his desires had been fulfilled.

* * *

45. Krishna and Balarama leave for Mathura

After taking His supper, Krishna came to bid goodnight to Akrura and asked him how Kamsa was dealing with Krishna's friends and relatives. He also inquired into Kamsa's plans. The Supreme Personality of Godhead then informed Akrura that his presence was very welcome. He inquired from him whether all his relatives and friends were well and free from all kinds of ailments. Krishna said He was very sorry that His maternal uncle, Kamsa, was the head of the kingdom:

"My father has undergone so much trouble simply because I am his son." Krishna said, "For this reason he has lost many other sons. I think Myself so fortunate that you have come as My friend and relative. My dear uncle Akrura, please tell Me the purpose of your visit to Vrindavana."

After this inquiry, Akrura explained everything, including Kamsa's attempt to kill Vasudeva, the father of Krishna. Akrura then explained that the purpose of his coming was to take Him and Balarama back to Mathura to be killed. After hearing all this Balarama and Krishna, who are expert at killing opponents, mildly laughed at the plans of Kamsa. They then informed Nanda Maharaja that Kamsa had invited all the cowherd men and boys to go to Mathura to participate in a special ceremony known as Dhanur-yajna (bow sacrifice). On Krishna's word, Nanda Maharaja at once called for the cowherd men and asked them to collect milk and all kinds of milk products to present to the King in the ceremony. He also sent instructions to the police chief of Vrindavana to tell all the inhabitants about Kamsa's invitation and that they were leaving the next morning.

When the *gopis* heard that Akrura had come to take Krishna and Balarama away to Mathura, they became overwhelmed with anxiety. Some of them became so aggrieved that their faces turned black and they began to breathe warmly and had palpitations of the heart. Others immediately fainted due to separation from Krishna. The *gopis* began to imagine the great functions in the city of Mathura. Krishna would pass through the streets, and the ladies and young girls of the city would see Him from the balconies of their houses. The *gopis* then began to condemn Akrura for taking Krishna away from them. They were also worried that Krishna may be more attracted to the young girls living in Mathura than to them.

The *gopis* prayed to the *devatas* to create some natural disturbance, such as a hurricane, storm or heavy rainfall, so that Krishna could not go to Mathura. The *gopis* cried all night before the departure of Krishna. As soon as the sun rose, Akrura finished his morning bath, got on the chariot and started for Mathura with Krishna and Balarama. Nanda Maharaja and the cowherd men got up on bullock carts after loading them with big earthen pots filled with yogurt, milk, *ghee* and other milk products, and then they began to follow the chariot of Krishna and Balarama. In spite of Krishna's asking the *gopis* not to obstruct their way, they all surrounded the chariot and stood on their toes to see Krishna with pitiable eyes. Krishna was greatly affected upon seeing the plight of the *gopis,* but His duty was to go to Mathura. He told them that they should not be upset since He was coming back very soon after finishing His business. The chariot set off and the *gopis* followed it with their eyes, watching the flag on the chariot as long as it was visible; finally they could see only dust in the distance. The *gopis* did not move from their places but stood until the chariot could not be seen at all. They remained standing still, as if they were painted pictures.

* * *

46. Akrura's Vision

The Lord, accompanied by Akrura and Balarama, travelled in the chariot with great speed towards the bank of the Yamuna. Krishna and Balarama took Their baths in the river and washed Their faces. After drinking the transparent, crystal-clear water of the Yamuna, They took Their seats again on the chariot. The chariot was standing underneath the shade of big trees, and the two brothers sat down there. Akrura then took Their permission to also take a bath in the Yamuna. According to Vedic ritual, after taking a bath in a river, one should stand at least half submerged and murmur the Gayatri mantra. While he was standing in the river, Akrura suddenly saw Balarama and Krishna within the water. He was surprised to see Them there because he was confident that They were sitting in the chariot where he left Them. Confused, he came out of the water and went to see where the boys were, only to be surprised again since They were both still sitting on the chariot as before. When he saw Them in the chariot, he began to wonder whether he had mistakenly seen Them in the water. He therefore went back to the river. This time he saw not only Balarama and Krishna but many of the devatas and other residents of the higher planets all bowing down before the Lord. He also saw Lord Sesha Naga, the serpent with thousands of hoods who is non-different from Lord Balarama. On the coiled lap of Sesha Naga, Akrura saw Krishna change into the smiling four armed form of Maha-Vishnu. He possessed dazzling beauty and His palms were like the lotus flower. Akrura then saw intimate servants of the Lord like the four Kumaras, Sunanda and Nanda, as well as *devatas* like Brahma and Lord Shiva. The nine great learned sages were there, and also devotees like Prahlada and Narada and the eight Vasus. All were engaged in offering prayers to the Lord with clean hearts and pure words. After seeing the transcendental Personality of Godhead, Akrura quickly became overwhelmed with joy and great devotion, and all over his body there was transcendental shivering. Although for the moment he was bewildered, he retained his clear consciousness and bowed down his head before the Lord. With folded hands and faltering voice, he also began to offer wonderful prayers to the Lord.

* * *

47. Krishna Enters Mathura

While Akrura was offering his prayers to the Supreme Personality of Godhead, the Lord disappeared from the water. Struck with wonder Akrura got out of the water and again approached the chariot. Krishna asked whether he had seen something wonderful within the water or in the sky. "My dear Lord, when I have seen You, what wonderful things have I not seen?" Akrura replied. After saying this, Akrura started driving the chariot, and by the end of the day they reached the precincts of Mathura. On their journey all the passers-by who saw Krishna and Balarama could not help but look at Them again and again.

In the meantime, the other inhabitants of Vrindavana, headed by Nanda and Upananda, had already reached Mathura by going through the forests, and they were awaiting the arrival of Krishna and Balarama in a garden. Upon reaching the entrance to Mathura, Krishna and Balarama got down from the chariot and shook hands with Akrura. Krishna informed him:

"You may go home now because We shall enter Mathura later, along with Our associates."

"My dear Lord," Akrura replied, "I cannot go to Mathura alone, leaving You aside. I am Your surrendered servant. Please come and sanctify my house."

"Akrura, I shall surely come to your home with My elder brother, Balarama, but only after killing all the demons who are envious of the Yadu dynasty. In this way I shall please all My relatives." Akrura became a little disappointed by these words of the Supreme Personality of Godhead, but he could not disobey the order. He therefore entered Mathura and informed Kamsa about the arrival of Krishna, and then he went home.

After Akrura's departure, Lord Krishna, Balarama and the cowherd boys entered Mathura to see the city. They saw that Mathura's city gates were well constructed from first-class marble, and that the doors were made of pure gold. There were gorgeous orchards and gardens all around, and the whole city was encircled by canals so that no enemy could easily enter. They saw that all the crossings of the roads were decorated with gold and that there were copper and brass storehouses for stocking grain. There were many rich men's houses, all appearing similarly designed, as if constructed by one engineer. The houses were decorated with costly jewels, and each and every one had fine gardens with fruit-bearing trees and flowers. The corridors and verandas of the houses were decorated with silk cloth and embroidery work in jewels and pearls. In front of the balcony windows were pigeons and peacocks walking and cooing. Over all the doors were decorations of fresh mango leaves and silk festoons.

When the news spread that Krishna, Balarama and the cowherd boys were within Mathura city, all the inhabitants gathered, and the ladies and girls went up to the roofs of the houses to see Them. They had been awaiting Krishna and Balarama's arrival with extreme eagerness. Thus in great haste, not even decorated or dressed properly, and dropping whatever they were doing, they went to see Krishna from the rooftops. When they actually saw Them, they took Krishna and Balarama within their hearts and began to embrace Them to their fullest desire and their bodily hairs stood up in ecstasy. They had heard of Krishna, but they had never seen Him, and now their longing was satisfied. The joyful ladies of Mathura then began to shower flowers upon Krishna and Balarama. When the brothers were passing through the streets, all the *brahmanas* in the neighbourhood also went out with sandal water and flowers and respectfully welcomed Them to the city. All the residents of Mathura began to talk among themselves about the elevated and pious activities of the people of Vrindavana. While Krishna and Balarama were passing in this way, They saw a washerman and dyer of clothing. Krishna asked him for some nice clothing, promising him all good fortune and happiness. Krishna was not a beggar, nor was He in need of clothing, but by this request He indicated that everyone should be ready to offer Him whatever He wants. That is the meaning of Krishna consciousness. Unfortunately, this washerman was a loyal servant of Kamsa and therefore could not appreciate the significance of Lord Krishna's request. This is the effect of bad association. The foolish washerman became very angry and refused the Lord's request:

"How can You be so impudent as to ask for clothing which belongs to our great King? Don't You dare do this again or You shall be punished. Anyone who unlawfully wants to use King Kamsa's property is always severely punished," said the washerman.

On hearing this, Lord Krishna became extremely angry, and He struck the washerman with His hand, separating the man's head from his body. The washerman's headless body collapsed to the ground. After this ghastly incident, the employees of the washerman quickly ran away, leaving all the King's clothing behind. Krishna and Balarama took possession of it and dressed according to Their choice; the rest of the clothes were offered to the cowherd boys. Krishna, Balarama and the boys then proceeded along the main road. Seeing all this, a devotee-tailor took the opportunity of service and quickly prepared some fine clothes for Krishna and Balarama. Krishna was most pleased with the tailor for this service, and gave him the benediction of *sarupya-mukti*, which meant that after leaving his body he would be liberated from birth and death and would attain a four-handed body exactly like that of Narayana in the Vaikuntha planets (the spiritual world). Krishna also declared that as long as he lived he would always earn plenty of money. By this incident Krishna proved that those who are Krishna conscious devotees will never lack materially or spiritually.

Now beautifully dressed, Krishna and Balarama went to visit a florist called Sudama. As soon as They reached the precinct of his house, the florist rushed out and with great devotion bowed down to offer his respectful obeisances. The florist offered a comfortable seat to Krishna and Balarama and asked his assistant to bring out fabulous flower garlands for Them both. He then offered other gifts and many humble prayers, all of which greatly satisfied the Lord. The florist begged only that he might remain Krishna's eternal servant, and through devotional service to the Lord do good to all living creatures. By this, it is clear that a devotee of the Lord should not be satisfied simply by his own spiritual advancement; he must be willing to work for the spiritual welfare of all others. Being satisfied with the florist, Lord Krishna not only gave him whatever benedictions he wanted, but over and above that He offered him all material opulences, family prosperity, a long duration of life and whatever else his heart desired within the material world.

* * *

48. The Breaking of the Bow

After leaving the florist's place, Krishna and Balarama saw a hunchbacked young woman carrying a dish of sandalwood pulp through the streets. Since Krishna is the reservoir of all pleasure, He wanted to make all His companions joyous by joking with the hunchbacked woman.

"O tall young woman," Krishna addressed her, "who are you? Tell Me, for whom are you carrying this sandalwood pulp in your hand? I think you should offer this sandalwood to Me, and if you do so I am sure you will be fortunate." Krishna is the Supreme Personality of Godhead, and so He knew everything about the hunchback. By His inquiry He indicated that there was no use in serving a demon; she would do better to serve Krishna and Balarama and get an immediate result for such service.

"My dear, beautiful, dark boy Krishna," the woman replied, "You may know that I am engaged as a maidservant of Kamsa. I am supplying him pulp of sandalwood daily. The King is very pleased with me for supplying this, but now I can understand that there is no one more worthy of receiving it than You two brothers."

Being captivated by the beautiful features of Krishna and Balarama, the hunchbacked woman began to smear the pulp over the upper portions of their bodies with great satisfaction and devotion. Now Krishna and Balarama had taken not only Kamsa's expensive clothes, but his finest sandalwood paste too. Krishna was most pleased by her service, and began to consider how best to reward her. He pressed the feet of the hunchbacked woman with His toes, and, capturing her cheeks with His fingers, gave her a jerk in order to make her back completely straight. At once the hunchbacked woman became beautiful. This incident shows that devotional service to Krishna is so potent that anyone who takes to it becomes qualified with all godly qualities. Krishna was attracted to the hunchbacked woman not for her beauty but for her service; as soon as she rendered service, she immediately became the most beautiful woman.

When the woman was turned by Krishna's favour into an exquisitely beautiful young girl, she frankly proposed to Krishna, "My dear hero, You must come to my place. I am very attracted to Your beauty, so I must receive You well." Krishna felt a little bit embarrassed in front of His elder brother, Balarama. He simply smiled at her words and, looking towards His cowherd boyfriends, He replied:

"My dear beautiful girl, I am especially pleased by your invitation, and I must come to your home after finishing My other business here." Krishna satisfied the girl in this way with sweet words. Leaving her there, He proceeded down the street of the marketplace, where the citizens were prepared to receive Him with various kinds of presentations, especially betel nuts, flowers and sandalwood pulp.

Kamsa had arranged for the sacrifice to take place in an arena with the large bow, which resembled a rainbow, supported near the sacrificial altar. This bow was protected by many constables and guards employed by King Kamsa. As Krishna and Balarama approached the bow, They were warned not to go any nearer, but Krishna ignored the warning. He forcibly went up and quickly took the big bow in His left hand. After stringing the bow in the presence of the crowd, He drew it back and broke it in half, exactly as an elephant easily breaks sugarcane. Everyone present appreciated Krishna's power. The loud sound of the bow cracking filled the air and was heard by Kamsa who began to fear for his life. The caretakers of the bow, who were standing by watching, became very angry, and with their respective weapons in hand they rushed towards Krishna, shouting, "Arrest Him! Arrest Him! Kill Him! Kill Him!" Krishna and Balarama were surrounded. But They also became angry, and taking up the two pieces of the broken bow, They began to beat off all of Kamsa's guards. While this turmoil was going on, Kamsa sent a small group of troops to assist the caretakers, but Krishna and Balarama fought with them also and killed them all.

After this, Krishna went out of the main gate and proceeded towards Their resting camp. Along the way, He visited various places in Mathura City with great delight. Seeing the activities and wonderful prowess of Krishna, all the astonished citizens of Mathura began to consider the two brothers to be *devatas*. The two brothers strolled carefree in the street, not caring for the law and order of Kamsa's city. As sunset approached, Krishna, Balarama and Their cowherd boyfriends went to the outskirts of the city where all their carts were assembled. They had certainly given Kamsa a clear hint of the severe danger that would be facing him the following day at the sacrifice.

* * *

49. Kamsa's Fear

When he learned the full extent of Krishna's activities that day, King Kamsa realised that the eighth son of Devaki had truly appeared and that now his death was imminent. Thinking of his impending demise, he could not sleep the entire night. He began to have many ominous visions, and see many strange and sinister omens, which all convinced him that Krishna and Balarama were his messengers of death. For example, when he looked in the mirror he could not see his own head. When he looked at the stars he saw everything doubled. He began to see holes in his shadow, and he could hear a high buzzing sound within his ears. All the trees before him appeared to be made of gold, and he could not see his own footprints in dust or muddy clay. In dreams he saw various kinds of ghosts being carried in a carriage drawn by donkeys. He also dreamed that someone gave him poison which he mistakenly drank. He then saw himself naked, wearing a garland of flowers, with his whole body smeared with oil as though in preparation for a funeral. All these signs made Kamsa sure he was soon to die. At the break of dawn he anxiously completed the arrangements for the wrestling match.

The wrestling arena was completely cleansed and decorated with flags and flowers, and the match was announced by the beating of drums. The fighting ring was quite beautiful due to so many streamers. Different types of viewing galleries were arranged for various kings, *brahmanas* and *kshatriyas*. The kings all had thrones especially reserved for them. Then Kamsa made his grand entrance and, accompanied by various ministers and secretaries, he sat on a raised platform especially meant for him. Although he was sitting amongst all his most powerful ministers, his heart was pounding in fear. Kamsa welcomed all the cowherd men from Vrindavana who presented him with the delicious milk products they had brought with them. The cowherd men also took their seats to one side of Kamsa on another platform especially meant for them.

When everything was ready, the wrestlers walked into the arena. Amongst the renowned fighters were Chanura, Mushtika, Shala and Toshala. Their huge bodies rippled with muscles as they strutted about the arena. These were the wrestlers who were meant to kill Krishna and Balarama.

* * *

50. Kuvalayapida

After taking Their baths, Krishna and Balarama heard the beating of the kettledrums in the wrestling camp, so they set off to see the fun. When They reached the main gate They were confronted by a large elephant called Kuvalayapida with a caretaker riding on it. Krishna could understand the purpose of the caretaker was to deliberately block their path, so He prepared Himself by tightening His clothes. He addressed the caretaker in a grave voice:

"You miscreant caretaker, give way and let Me pass through the gate. If you block My way, I shall send you and your elephant to the kingdom of death."

The caretaker became angry, and in order to challenge Krishna, as was previously planned, he provoked the elephant to attack. The elephant then rushed towards Krishna and tried to catch Him with its trunk, but Krishna nimbly moved behind the elephant. The elephant could only see to the end of its trunk, and so could not see Krishna hiding behind its legs, but still it tried again to capture Him with its trunk. Krishna ran behind the elephant and caught its tail and began to drag it with great strength for at least twenty-five yards. Krishna pulled the elephant from this side to that, from right to left, just as He used to pull a calf by its tail in His childhood. After this, Krishna went in front of the elephant and gave it a strong slap. He then slipped away from the elephant's view and ran to its back again. Then, falling down on the ground, Krishna placed Himself in front of the elephant's two hind legs and caused it to trip and fall. Krishna immediately got up, but the elephant, thinking that He was still lying down, tried to push an ivory tusk through the body of Krishna by forcibly stabbing it into the ground. Although the elephant was harassed and angry, the caretaker riding on its head tried to provoke it further. The elephant then rushed madly towards Krishna. As soon as it came within reach, Krishna caught hold of its trunk and pulled the elephant down. When the elephant and caretaker fell, Krishna jumped up on the elephant, broke off one of its tusks, and with it killed both the elephant and the caretaker.

After killing the elephant, Krishna took the ivory tusk on His shoulder. Decorated with drops of perspiration and sprinkled with the blood of the elephant, He looked very beautiful, and thus He proceeded towards the wrestling arena. Lord Balarama took the other tusk of the elephant on His shoulder. When Krishna entered the arena everyone saw Him differently according to their individual relationship with Him. He appeared to the wrestlers exactly like a powerful thunderbolt. To the people in general He appeared as the most beautiful personality and to the ladies He appeared to be the most attractive man. The cowherd men saw Him as their kinsman and the impious *kshatriya* kings saw Him as the strongest ruler and their chastiser. To the parents of Krishna, Nanda and Yashoda, He appeared to be the most loving child. But to Kamsa, the king of the Bhoja dynasty, Krishna appeared to be death personified.

Having heard that Krishna had already killed the

elephant Kuvalayapida, Kamsa knew beyond doubt that Krishna was formidable, and therefore realized he was in grave danger.   The famous wrestler Chanura then began to talk with Krishna and Balarama.

"My dear Krishna and Balarama," he said, "we have heard about Your past activities. You are great heroes, and therefore the King has called You here. We have heard that Your arms are very strong and that while tending Your cows in the forest You enjoy wrestling with each other. We wish, therefore, for You to join with us in wrestling so that all the people present here, along with the King, can see just how good you are, and thus be pleased."

"This offer of wrestling is a great favour upon us," Krishna replied, "but the fact is that We are simply small boys. We sometimes play in the forests of Vrindavana with Our friends who are Our own age. We think that to fight children of equal age and strength is good for Us, but to be made to fight great wrestlers like you would not be appreciated by the audience."

"My dear Krishna," Chanura replied, "You have already killed the elephant Kuvalyapida, who was capable of fighting thousands of other elephants, so please do not pretend You are just ordinary boys. Because of Your strength, it is your duty to compete with the strongest wrestlers amongst us. I therefore wish to wrestle with You, and Your elder brother, Balarama, will wrestle with Mushtika."

* * *

51. The Killing of Kamsa

After Kamsa's wrestlers expressed their determination to fight, the Supreme Personality of Godhead confronted Chanura, and Lord Balarama confronted Mushtika. Krishna and Chanura, and then Balarama and Mushtika locked themselves hand to hand, leg to leg, and each began to press hard against the other. They joined palm to palm, calf to calf, head to head, chest to chest and began to strike each other. The fighting increased as they pushed each other from one place to another. One captured the other and threw him down on the ground, and another rushed from the back to the front of another and tried to overcome him with a hold. There was picking up, dragging and pushing, and then the legs and hands were locked together. All the arts of wrestling were perfectly exhibited by the parties, as each tried his best to defeat his opponent.

As Krishna had predicted, the audience in the wrestling arena were not at all happy since they thought the match completely unfair. They considered Krishna and Balarama to be mere boys before Chanura and Mushtika, who were the strongest wrestlers, and were as solid as stone. Being compassionate and favouring Krishna and Balarama, the many ladies in the audience began to talk as follows:

"Dear friends, there is injustice here." Another said, "Even in front of the King this wrestling is going on between unequal sides."

As the Supersoul within the heart of every living being, Krishna understood that the ladies in the assembly, along with Nanda Maharaja, Yashoda, Vasudeva and Devaki were all anxious for His safety - not knowing He was unlimitedly strong. He therefore decided not to continue wrestling, but to kill the wrestlers immediately. Lord Krishna struck Chanura three times with His fist, causing him to jolt backwards, much to the astonishment of the audience. Chanura then took his last chance and attacked Krishna by folding his two hands and striking Krishna's chest. Lord Krishna was no more disturbed by this than an elephant hit by a flower garland. Krishna quickly caught the two hands of Chanura and began to wheel him around, and just by this the mighty wrestler lost his life. Krishna then threw him to the ground, scattering his ornaments hither and thither.

Mushtika also struck Balarama, and Balarama returned the stroke with great force. Mushtika began to tremble and vomit blood, and then fell down just like a tree in a hurricane. After the two wrestlers were killed, another one named Kuta came forward. Lord Balarama straight away caught him in His left hand and casually killed him. Another large wrestler called Shala came forward, and Krishna swiftly cracked his head with a kick. Then Toshala came forward and was killed in the same way. Thus all the great wrestlers were killed by Krishna and Balarama, and those left alive fled from the arena in fear. All the cowherd boyfriends of Krishna and Balarama approached Them and congratulated Them with great pleasure. While trumpets resounded and drums were beaten, the leg bells on the feet of Krishna and Balarama tinkled.

Only Kamsa was morose; he neither clapped nor offered blessings to Krishna. Kamsa resented the fact that the trumpets and drums were being played for Krishna's victory, and he was sorry that his best wrestlers had been killed or had run away. He therefore ordered the band to stop playing and addressed his men as follows:

"I order that these two sons of Vasudeva be immediately driven out of Mathura. The cowherd boys who have come with Them should be robbed and all their riches taken away. Nanda Maharaja should now be arrested and killed for his cunning behaviour, and that rascal Vasudeva should also be killed without delay. Also my father, Ugrasena, who has always supported my enemies against my will, should now be executed, killed, all of them killed."

Before the guards could move, Lord Krishna, who became furious at Kamsa's orders, jumped onto the high dais of King Kamsa. Kamsa was expecting Krishna's attack, and he quickly unsheathed his sword which he wielded up and down and side to side in an effort to keep Krishna away. But it was to no avail. The supremely powerful Lord caught hold of Kamsa with great force, knocked the sword from his hand, the crown from his head and then grabbed his long hair. Krishna then dragged Kamsa from his high throne, down the steps and then threw him into the wrestling arena. Then Krishna jumped into the arena, straddled Kamsa's chest and began to strike him over and over again with his fists. Simply from the blows of Krishna's fist, Kamsa lost his life. To assure His parents that Kamsa was really dead, Lord Krishna dragged his lifeless body around the arena just as a lion drags an elephant after killing it. When the packed arena saw this, there was a great roaring sound from all sides as some spectators expressed their joy and others cried in sorrow.

From the day Kamsa heard he would be killed by the eighth son of Devaki, he was always thinking of Krishna twenty-four hours a day, without stopping—even while eating, walking and breathing—and so after being killed by Krishna he was blessed with liberation from the material world. In the *Bhagavad-gita* it is stated, *sada tad-bhava-bhavitah:* [Bg. 8.6] a person gets his next life according to the thoughts in which he is always absorbed. Kamsa was constantly thinking of Krishna in his form of Narayana holding the deadly Sudarshana disc, and so at the time of death he attained the same form as Narayana in the spiritual world.

Kamsa had eight brothers, headed by Kanka, all of them younger than he, and when they learned that their elder brother had been killed, they combined together and rushed towards Krishna in great anger to slay Him. To spare Krishna having to kill more of His uncles, Balarama took charge of killing them. He took up a weapon and killed the eight brothers one after another, just as a lion kills a flock of deer. Krishna and Balarama thus proved true the statement that the Supreme Personality of Godhead appears in order to give protection to the pious and to kill the impious demons.

* * *

52. Krishna Frees His Relatives

After this great victory the *devatas* from the higher planetary systems showered flowers, congratulating Krishna and Balarama. The wives of Kamsa and his eight brothers were aggrieved at the sudden death of their husbands, and all of them struck their foreheads and shed torrents of tears. Crying loudly and embracing the bodies of their dead husbands, the wives of Kamsa and his brothers said:

"Our dear husbands, without you we are nothing. We know that Lord Krishna is the supreme master and supreme enjoyer of everything; therefore, one who neglects His authority can never be happy and will ultimately be punished by cruel death, just as you have been."

Krishna tried to comfort His aunts the best He could, and then, since He was the nephew of all the dead princes, He performed the death ceremonies. Krishna and Balarama then released Their father and mother, Vasudeva and Devaki, from Kamsa's prison. Krishna and Balarama fell at Their parents' feet and offered them prayers. Although Krishna was born as their son, Vasudeva and Devaki were always conscious of His supreme position. At this point Krishna covered them with His special, illusory energy so they would see Him just as their little child, and not as God.

"My dear father and mother," Krishna said, "a man cannot repay his debt to his parents from whom he gets this human form of life. It is only this human form which gives us the possibility of gaining liberation from material existence. If a person is able to care for or give protection to old parents, a chaste wife, children, the spiritual master, *brahmanas* and other dependents but does not do so, he is considered already dead, although he is supposedly breathing. My dear father and mother, you have always been anxious for Our protection, but unfortunately We could not render any service to you. Until now We have simply wasted Our time; please excuse Us for Our sinfulness."

When the Supreme Personality of Godhead was speaking as an innocent boy in very sweet words, Vasudeva and Devaki became captivated by parental affection and silently embraced Him and Balarama with great pleasure and affection, shedding torrents of tears. Vasudeva and Devaki had suffered so much trouble from Kamsa just because Krishna was their son, but now they had been set free and were finally reunited with their beloved children. Having consoled His father and mother, Krishna then approached His grandfather Ugrasena, who Kamsa had also arrested and imprisoned, and announced that he would now be the King of the Yadu kingdom. Krishna said to him:

"My dear grandfather, out of fear of My late uncle Kamsa, all the kings belonging to the Yadu, Vrishni, Andhaka, Madhu, Dasarha and Kukura dynasties were very anxious and disturbed. Now you can pacify them all and give them assurance of security. The whole kingdom will be peaceful under your rule."

On account of good government in the presence of Krishna and Balarama, the inhabitants of Mathura felt complete satisfaction and the whole world did indeed become peaceful once more.

* * *

53. Learning from Their Spiritual Master

After some time, Nanda Maharaja and Yashoda, who were living in Mathura to be with Krishna and Balarama, decided they wanted to go back to their home in Vrindavana. Krishna and Balarama spoke to them as follows:

"Dear father and mother, although We were born of Vasudeva and Devaki, you have been Our real father and mother, because from Our very birth and childhood you raised Us with great affection and love. We know you will feel separation from us when you return to Vrindavana, but please rest assured that We shall join you there after giving some satisfaction to Vasudeva and Devaki, and Our grandfather and other family members." Krishna and Balarama thus satisfied Nanda and Yashoda by kind words and by gifts of clothing, ornaments and copper utensils.

After this, Vasudeva had his sons initiated by sacred thread. During the ceremony, Vasudeva remembered the cows he had wanted to give in charity to the *brahmanas* after the birth of Krishna and Balarama. Being imprisoned by Kamsa at that time he had been able to do so, only within his mind. With the death of Kamsa, his herds were released, and he was now free to give real cows to the *brahmanas*. When Balarama and Krishna were initiated by their family priest, Garga Muni, They both chanted the

Gayatri mantra.

It is customary, after being initiated, for one to live away from home for some time under the care of the *acharya* (spiritual master) to be trained in spiritual life. During this period, one has to work under the spiritual master as an ordinary menial servant, following many rules and regulations. Krishna and Balarama strictly followed this system while living under the instruction of their own spiritual master, Sandipani Muni, who was a resident of Avantipura, in the northern Indian district of Ujjain. According to the Vedic literatures a spiritual master should be respected and regarded on an equal level with the Supreme Personality of Godhead. Krishna and Balarama set the perfect example for everyone by following those principles with great enthusiasm. Because Krishna and Balarama happened to be *kshatriyas*, They were trained in military science, politics and ethics. Politics includes such departments of knowledge as how to make peace, how to fight, how to pacify, how to divide and rule and how to give shelter.

After hearing only once from Their teacher, Krishna and Balarama learned all the arts and sciences, required in human society in sixty-four days. During the day They took lessons on a particular subject from their teacher, and by nightfall They were expert in that department of knowledge.

Firstly They learned how to sing, how to compose songs and how to recognize different tunes; how to sing and dance to different kinds of rhythms and melodies, and how to follow them by beating different kinds of drums. They learned how to write dramas, and all about painting. They learned how to set valuable jewels in ornaments. They learned the art of producing melodious sounds from water pots, by filling a number of them to different levels so that when hit they produced different tones. They learned how to decorate temples with flowers, an art involving a small, aromatic fountain of flowers, which is still practiced to this day in Vrindavana during the summer season.

Krishna and Balarama learned the art of dressing hair in various styles and fixing a helmet in different positions on the head. They also learned how to set up a theatrical stage, how to decorate dramatic actors with clothes, and how to sprinkle sandalwood pulp and water to produce a nice fragrance. They also learned the art of performing magical feats. Within the magical field there is an art by which a person dresses himself in such a way that when he approaches a friend he cannot be recognized. Krishna and Balarama also learned how to make various syrups and drinks. They also learned different types of sewing and embroidery work, as well as how to manipulate thin threads for dancing puppets. This art includes how to string wires on musical instruments, such as the *vina, sitar* and *tamboura*, to produce melodious sounds. Then They learned how to make and solve riddles. They learned the art of how even a dull student can quickly learn the alphabet and read books. Then They learned how to rehearse and act out a drama. They also studied the art of solving crossword puzzles, filling up the missing spaces and making complete words.

They also learned how to draw and read illustrated

literature whereby stories are represented by pictures. Krishna and Balarama also learned the art of architecture—how to construct residential buildings. They learned to recognize valuable jewels by studying their lustre and colours. Then They learned the art of placing jewels in a gold and silver setting so that they look very beautiful. They also learned how to study soil to find minerals. They learned to study herbs and plants to discover how they would act as medicine for different ailments. By studying the different species of plants, They learned how to crossbreed plants and trees and get different types of fruits. They then learned how to teach parrots to speak and answer questions.

They learned practical psychology—how to influence another's mind and thus induce another to act according to one's own desire. (Sometimes this is called hypnotism). They learned how to wash hair, dye it in different colours and curl it in different ways. They learned the art of telling what is written in someone's book without actually seeing it. They learned to tell what is contained in another's fist.

Krishna and Balarama learned how to speak and understand the languages of various countries. Not only did They learn the languages of human beings but also how to speak with animals and birds. Then They learned how to make carriages and airplanes from flowers. (It is said in the Ramayana that after defeating Ravana, Ramachandra was carried from Lanka to Ayodhya on a plane of flowers, called a *pushpa-ratha*). Krishna and Balarama then learned the art of foretelling events by seeing signs or omens. For example, if while leaving one's home one sees a person with a bucket full of water, that is supposed to be a good sign. But if one sees someone with an empty bucket, it is not a good sign. Similarly, if one sees a cow being milked alongside its calf, that is also a good sign. The result of understanding these signs is that one can foretell events, and Krishna and Balarama learned this science. Krishna and Balarama learned the art of cutting valuable stones such as diamonds, and They learned how to satisfy one's desires and how to free oneself from unreasonable desires.

All these interesting arts and sciences were learnt by Krishna and Balarama whilst staying in their spiritual master's ashram.

* * *

54. Krishna Rescues the Son
of His Teacher

After they had learned all these things, Lord Krishna and Balarama offered to serve Their teacher by awarding him anything he desired. This offering by the student to the spiritual master is called *guru-dakshina*. It is essential that a student satisfy the teacher in return for any learning received, either material or spiritual. When Krishna and Balarama offered Their service in this way, the teacher, Sandipani Muni, thought it wise to ask Them for something extraordinary, something no common student could offer. He therefore consulted with his wife about what to request. He and his wife had already seen the extraordinary potencies of Krishna and Balarama and could understand that the two boys were the Supreme Personality of Godhead. They therefore decided to ask for the return of their son, who had previously drowned in the ocean near the shore at Prabhasa-kshetra.

When Krishna and Balarama heard from Their teacher about the death of his son, They quickly set off for Prabhasa-kshetra on Their chariot. Reaching the beach, They asked the controlling deity of the ocean to return the son of Their teacher. The ocean deity instantly appeared before the Lord and offered Him respectful obeisances with great humility. The Lord said:

"Some time back you caused the drowning of the son

of Our teacher. I order you to return him."

"The boy was not actually taken by me but was captured by a demon named Panchajana." The ocean deity replied, "This great demon generally remains deep in the water in the shape of a conchshell. The son of Your teacher might be within the belly of that demon, having been devoured by him."

On hearing this, Krishna dived deep into the water and caught hold of the demon Panchajana. He killed him on the spot but could not find the son of His teacher within his belly. Therefore He took the demon's dead body and returned to His chariot on the beach of Prabhasa-kshetra. From there He started for the residence of Yamaraja, the superintendent of death. When Krishna arrived there he blew on His conchshell.

Yamaraja understood perfectly who Krishna and Balarama were, and therefore he immediately offered his obeisances and humble service to the Lord. Lord Sri Krishna then asked him to return His teacher's son. Yamaraja returned the boy to the Supreme Personality of Godhead and Krishna and Balarama brought him to his father. The brothers asked if Their teacher had anything more to ask from Them, but Sandipani Muni replied:

"My dear sons, You have done enough for me. I am now completely satisfied. What further want can there be for a man who has disciples like You? My dear boys, You may now go home. These glorious acts of Yours will always be renowned all over the world. You are above all blessing, yet it is my duty to bless You. I therefore give You the benediction that whatever You speak will remain as eternally fresh as the instructions of the *Vedas*. Your teachings will be honoured not only within this universe or in this millennium but in all places and ages and will remain increasingly new and important."

Due to this benediction from His teacher, Lord Krishna's *Bhagavad-gita* is increasingly fresh and is renowned not only within this universe but in other planets and other universes also.

Being so ordered by Their teacher, Krishna and Balarama swiftly returned home on Their chariot. All the residents of Mathura, who had not seen Krishna and Balarama for a long time, were very pleased to see Them again. They felt joyful, like a person who has regained some cherished lost property.

* * *

55. Uddhava Visits Vrindavana

Nanda Maharaja returned to Vrindavana without Krishna and Balarama, accompanied only by the cowherd boys and men. When Krishna was leaving for Mathura on the chariot driven by Akrura, the *gopis* had blocked His way. At that time Krishna assured them that He was coming back just after finishing His business in Mathura. He told them not to be overwhelmed and in this way pacified them. It seemed on the face of it that Krishna had broken His promise. However, although the inhabitants of Vrindavana felt separation from Krishna, the resulting *bhava* (ecstasy) caused them to perceive that Krishna was always present with them by His *lila*, or pastimes. So Krishna did return in the form of this special type of ecstasy.

As the *gopis* were thinking of Krishna in separation twenty-four hours a day, so Krishna was also always thinking of the *gopis*, mother Yashoda, Nanda Maharaja and the other residents of Vrindavana. Although He appeared to be away from them, He could understand how they were transcendentally aggrieved, and so He wanted to send Uddhava to give them a message of solace. Uddhava was a great friend of Krishna's, and was very intelligent and highly qualified. He also had a beautiful form just like Krishna's. It was Krishna's special favour to Uddhava to send him since he would be able to study, first hand, the great love for Krishna experienced by the residents of Vrindavana.

Thus requested by Lord Krishna, Uddhava left on his chariot with the message, reaching Vrindavana at sunset, when the cows were returning home from the pasturing ground. Uddhava entered the house of Nanda Maharaja, who offered him a comfortable sitting place.

"My dear Uddhava," Nanda Maharaja said, "how is my friend Vasudeva enjoying life? He is now released from the prison of Kamsa, and is back with his friends and his children, Krishna and Balarama. He must be very happy. Tell me about him and his welfare. We are so happy that Kamsa, the most sinful demon, has been killed." Nanda Maharaja then described how much they all missed Krishna and Balarama, and how they were thinking about Their pastimes day and night.

"My dear mother Yashoda and Nanda Maharaja," Uddhava replied, "you are most respectable among human beings because no one but you can meditate in such transcendental ecstasy. Krishna promised that He would come back to Vrindavana after finishing His business in Mathura. This promise He will surely fulfil. I therefore request the two of you not to be unhappy on account of Krishna's absence."

Nanda and Uddhava thus passed the whole night discussing Krishna.

* * *

56. Krishna's Message to the Gopis

When the *gopis* saw Uddhava the following day, they thought he looked almost exactly like Krishna, and from this they realised he must be a great devotee of Krishna. They began to contemplate, "Who is this boy who looks just like Krishna? He has the same eyes like lotus petals, the same raised nose and beautiful face, and he is smiling in the same way. Where has this boy come from? Who is the fortunate girl who has him for her husband?" They were most anxious to know everything about Uddhava, and because they were simple village girls they completely surrounded him. When the *gopis* understood that Uddhava had a message from Krishna, they became very happy and invited him to sit with them in a quiet place so they could talk freely.

Uddhava could see that the *gopis* of Vrindavana were all completely absorbed in thoughts of Krishna and His childhood activities. Srimati Radharani was so absorbed in thoughts of Krishna that She actually began to talk with a bumblebee which was flying there and trying to touch Her lotus feet. While the other *gopis* were talking with Uddhava, Srimati Radharani took that bumblebee to be another messenger from Krishna and began to talk with it as follows:

"Bumblebee, you are accustomed to drinking honey from flower to flower, and therefore you have chosen to be a messenger of Krishna, who is of the same nature as you. You have come here carrying a message for Me, anxious to touch My feet. But My dear bumblebee, let Me warn you—don't touch Me! I don't want any messages from your unreliable master. You are the unreliable servant of an unreliable master." It may be that Srimati Radharani spoke like this in order to indirectly criticize the messenger Uddhava for being another unreliable servant of the unreliable master, Krishna. She again addressed the bumblebee, "Your master Krishna is exactly like you. You sit down on a flower, and after taking a little honey you fly away and sit in another flower and taste again. Once Krishna gave Me the chance to enjoy His company, and then He left us altogether. We are not going to be cheated anymore by Krishna or His messengers. Krishna is now in the city and is better known as the friend of Arjuna. He now has many new girlfriends, who are no doubt very happy in His association. You are just trying to pacify Me by your behaviour as a flatterer, and therefore you have put your head at My feet. But I know the trick you are trying to play. I know that you are a messenger coming from an even greater trickster, Krishna. Therefore, please leave Me."

Since Krishna is absolute, His so-called unkind activities are as pleasing as His kind activities. Therefore saintly persons and great devotees like the *gopis* cannot give up Krishna in any circumstance. Lord Chaitanya, the most recent incarnation of Krishna, therefore prayed, "Krishna, You are free and independent in all respects. You can either embrace Me or crush Me under Your feet—whatever You like. You may make Me broken-hearted by not letting Me see You throughout My whole life, but You are My only object of love."

"In My opinion," Srimati Radharani continued, "no one should hear about Krishna, because as soon as a drop of the nectar of His transcendental activities is poured into the ear, one immediately gives up attachment for this material world, including family, home, wife, children and everything else. This makes his relatives and himself unhappy. Then he wanders in search of Krishna and chooses to become a poor mendicant. Please do not talk any more about Krishna. It is better to talk about something else. We are already doomed, like the black-spotted she-deer in the forest who are enchanted by the sweet musical vibration of the hunter." These talks of Radharani with the bumblebee messenger, in which She both criticises Krishna and at the same time proves herself incapable of giving Him up, are signs of the topmost transcendental ecstasy, called *maha-bhava*.

In the meantime, the bee, flying hither and thither, appeared before Her again. She thought, "Krishna is still kind to Me. In spite of the messenger's carrying my disturbing messages, He is so compassionate that He has again sent the bee to take Me to Him." Thinking that the bee had come to take her to Krishna, Srimati Radharani was careful this time not to say anything against Him:

"My dear friend, I welcome you," She said. "Krishna is so kind that He has again sent you back, in spite of your carrying My message against Him. All good fortune to you My dear friend. You have come to take Me to Krishna because He is not able to come here, being surrounded by new girlfriends in Mathura. But you are a tiny creature. How can you take Me there?"

All this time Uddhava had been standing nearby and so had heard Radharani talking in this way. He was amazed at how the *gopis* thought of Krishna constantly in that topmost ecstasy of divine *maha-bhava* love. He had brought a message in writing from Krishna, and now he wanted to present it to the *gopis*.

"My dear *gopis*, your mission of human life is now successful. You are all wonderful devotees of the Supreme Personality of Godhead. This love you have developed for Krishna is very, very difficult to attain, even for great sages and saintly persons. I think myself most fortunate that I have been favoured, by your grace, to see you in this condition." When Uddhava said that he had a message from Krishna, the *gopis* were much more interested in hearing the message than hearing about their own exalted position. Uddhava took out the letter to read it: "These are the words of the Personality of Godhead. 'My dear *gopis*, My dear friends, please know that separation between ourselves is impossible at any time, at any place or under any circumstances, because I am all-pervading. Nothing is separate from Me. Knowledge of the Absolute is no longer necessary for you since you have loved Me from the very beginning of your lives.' "

After Uddhava had finished, the *gopis* asked him all about Krishna's activities and His great victory over Kamsa. They also asked him if Krishna still remembered them, and whether He would be coming back to Vrindavana. After staying in Vrindavana for some time, Uddhava desired to go back to Krishna, and so he begged permission to leave from Nanda Maharaja and Yashoda. He had a farewell meeting with the *gopis*, and, taking permission from them also, he mounted his chariot to start for Mathura. All the inhabitants of Vrindavana, headed by Maharaja Nanda and Yashoda, came to bid him good-bye and presented him with valuable gifts. When Uddhava had been sufficiently honoured and worshiped by the pure devotees of Vrindavana, he returned to Mathura and to his master, Krishna. After offering respects by bowing down before Lord Krishna and Balarama, he described the wonderful devotional life of the inhabitants of Vrindavana. He then presented all the gifts given by the inhabitants of Vrindavana to Vasudeva, the father of Krishna, and Ugrasena, Krishna's grandfather.

* * *

57. Krishna Pleases His Devotees

For days together, Krishna heard from Uddhava all the details of his visit to Vrindavana, especially the condition of His father and mother and of the *gopis* and the cowherd boys. Lord Krishna was fully satisfied that Uddhava was able to solace them by his instructions and by the message delivered to them. Lord Krishna then decided to go with Uddhava to the house of Kubja, the hunchback woman who had pleased Him by offering Him sandalwood pulp when He was entering the city of Mathura. When Kubja saw that Lord Krishna had come to her house to fulfil His promised visit, she quickly got up from her chair to receive Him warmly. Accompanied by her many girlfriends, she began to talk with Him with great respect and honour. After offering Him a nice place to sit, she worshiped Lord Krishna in a manner just suitable to her position. Uddhava was similarly received by Kubja and her girlfriends, but he did not want to sit on an equal level with Krishna and thus simply sat down on the floor. After satisfying Kubja and offering her sweet words, Krishna returned home with Uddhava.

After a while, Krishna also fulfilled His promise to visit Akrura's home. When Krishna, Balarama and Uddhava approached the house of Akrura, he came out and embraced Uddhava and offered respectful obeisances, bowing down before Lord Krishna and Balarama. Krishna, Balarama and Uddhava offered him obeisances in turn and were offered appropriate sitting places. When all were comfortably seated, Akrura washed their feet and sprinkled the water on his head. Then he offered nice clothing, flowers and sandalwood pulp in regular worship. All three of them were completely satisfied by Akrura's behaviour. Akrura then bowed down before Krishna, putting his head on the ground. Then, placing Krishna's lotus feet on his lap, Akrura gently began to massage them. Akrura's eyes filled with tears of love for Krishna, and he began to offer many wonderful prayers:

"My dear Akrura," Krishna said when Akrura had finished, "you are forever Our friend and well-wisher. You are always ready to act for Our welfare. Kindly, therefore, go to Hastinapura and see what arrangement has been made for the Pandavas." Krishna was anxious to know about the sons of Pandu (who were all His devotees) because at a very young age they had lost their father. Krishna continued: "I have heard that after King Pandu's death, his young sons—Yudhisthira, Bhima, Arjuna, Nakula and Sahadeva— along with their widowed mother, have come under the charge of Dhritarashtra, who is supposed to look after them as their guardian. But I have also heard that Dhritarashtra is not only blind from birth but also blind in his affection for his cruel son Duryodhana. The five Pandavas are the sons of King Pandu, but Dhritarashtra, due to Duryodhana's plans and designs, is not favourably disposed towards them. Kindly go and study how Dhritarashtra is dealing with the Pandavas. On receipt of your report, I shall consider how to help them." In this way the Supreme Personality of Godhead, Krishna, ordered Akrura to go to Hastinapura, and then He returned home, accompanied by Balarama and Uddhava.

* * *

58. The Ill-motivated Dhritarashtra

Thus ordered by the Supreme Personality of Godhead, Sri Krishna, Akrura visited Hastinapura, said to be the site of what is now New Delhi. The part of New Delhi still known as Indraprastha is accepted by people in general as the old capital of the Pandavas. The name Hastinapura suggests that the Pandavas kept many *hastis*, or elephants, in the capital. Keeping elephants is very expensive; so to keep many elephants meant that the kingdom was extremely wealthy. Hastinapura, as Akrura saw when he reached it, was full of elephants, horses, chariots and other opulences. At that time the kings of Hastinapura ruled the whole world. Their fame was widely spread throughout the entire kingdom, and their administration was conducted under the good advice of learned *brahmanas*.

After seeing the opulent capital city, Akrura met King Dhritarashtra who was sitting with grandfather Bhishma. After meeting them, he went to see Vidura and then Kunti, Akrura's cousin. One after another, he saw King Bahlika and his son Somadatta, Dronacharya, Kripacharya, Karna and Duryodhana. Then he saw the son of Dronacharya, Ashvatthama, as well as the five Pandava brothers and other friends and relatives living in the city. All the time Akrura carefully studied the political situation so he would be able to give Krishna a full report of how the Pandavas were being treated. As it happened, Dhritarashtra was unlawfully occupying the throne after the death of King Pandu, despite the presence of Pandu's sons (the Pandavas). Akrura could understand very well that the ill-motivated Dhritarashtra favoured his own sons over those of his brother Pandu. In fact, having stolen the kingdom, Dhritarashtra was now planning to get rid of the five Pandava brothers altogether. Akrura knew that all the sons of Dhritarashtra, headed by Duryodhana, were crooked politicians. Dhritarashtra did not act in accordance with the good instructions given by Bhishma and Vidura; instead, he was acting under the bad directions of such persons as Karna and Shakuni. Akrura decided to stay in Hastinapura for a few months to study the whole situation thoroughly.

Gradually Akrura learned from Kunti and Vidura that the sons of Dhritarashtra were intolerant and envious of the five Pandava brothers because of their extraordinary learning in military science and their greatly developed bodily strength. The Pandavas acted as truly chivalrous heroes, exhibited all the good qualities of *kshatriyas* and were very responsible princes, always thinking of the welfare of the citizens. Akrura also learned that the envious sons of Dhritarashtra had tried to kill the Pandavas by poisoning them.

Akrura happened to be one of the cousins of Kunti, the mother of the five Pandava brothers; therefore when they met she began to inquire about her relatives. She especially inquired about Krishna and Balarama, her glorious nephews.

"Does Krishna, the Supreme Personality of Godhead, who is very affectionate to His devotees, remember my sons?" asked Kunti, "Does Balarama remember us?" Inside, Kunti felt like a she-deer in the midst of hungry tigers. After the death of her husband, King Pandu, she was supposed to take care of the five Pandava children, but the sons of Dhritarashtra were always planning to kill them. Being a devotee of Lord Krishna, she always thought of Him and expected that one day Krishna would come and save them from their dangerous position. She inquired from Akrura as to whether Krishna was planning to come and advise her sons on how to escape the sinister plotting of Dhritarashtra and his sons. Talking with Akrura about all these affairs, she felt helpless and exclaimed, "My dear Krishna, my dear Krishna! You are the real well-wisher of the whole universe. I am now grief-stricken with my five fatherless sons. I can fully understand that, but for Your lotus feet, there is no shelter or protection in this world. Please accept me as Your fully surrendered devotee."

Although Krishna was not present, Kunti offered her prayers to Him as if she were seeing Him face to face. Krishna does not have to be physically present everywhere since He is actually present everywhere by His spiritual potency. When Kunti was offering her prayers she could not check herself and began to cry loudly before Akrura. Vidura was also present, and both Akrura and Vidura began to solace her by glorifying her five sons, namely Yudhishtira, Arjuna, Bhima, Nakula and Sahadeva. They pacified her, saying that her sons were extraordinarily powerful since they were born of great *devatas* like

Yamaraja, Indra and Vayu.

Akrura decided to return and report on the strained circumstances in which he found Kunti and her five sons. He first wanted to give good advice to Dhritarashtra, who was so favourably inclined toward his own sons and so unfavourably inclined toward the Pandavas. When King Dhritarashtra was sitting among friends and relatives, Akrura began to address him:

"My dear son of Vichitravirya, you have unlawfully taken the throne of the Pandavas. I beg to advise you that since you are now in any case the ruler, please at least rule the kingdom on moral and ethical principles. If you do so, and treat everyone fairly, your name and fame will carry on forever. Even if you do not allow the Pandavas to rule, then at least think of their welfare as though they were your own sons. But if you do not follow this principle, you will be unpopular among your subjects, and in the next life you will have to live in a hellish condition. I therefore hope you will treat your sons and the sons of Pandu equally."

"My dear Akrura," Dhritarashtra replied, "you are very charitable in giving me good instructions, but unfortunately I cannot accept them even though I can see they are valuable. Unfortunately, they do not stay in my flickering mind, just as the glittering lightning in the sky does not stay fixed in a cloud. I can understand only that no one can stop the onward progress of the supreme will. I understand that the Supreme Personality of Godhead, Krishna, has appeared in the family of the Yadus to decrease the troublesome load on this earth."

After hearing him speak, Akrura could clearly

understand that Dhritarashtra was not going to change his policy of discriminating against the Pandavas in favour of his sons. He at once took leave of his friends in Hastinapura and returned to his home in the kingdom of the Yadus where he clearly explained the whole situation to Lord Krishna and Balarama.

* * *

Our Founder & Acharya
Srila Prabhupada
A Brief Life Sketch

According to the Vedic literatures, the most recent incarnation of Lord Krishna appeared just over five hundred years ago as Sri Chaitanya Mahaprabhu, the Golden *Avatara,* in Mayapur, West Bengal. It was Lord Chaitanya who predicted that the chanting of His holy names - **Hare Krishna, Hare Krishna, Krishna Krishna, Hare Hare, Hare Rama, Hare Rama, Rama Rama, Hare Hare** - would spread beyond the shores of India to every town and village of the world. The person who eventually made this prophecy come true was His Divine Grace A.C. Bhaktivedanta Swami Prabhupada (Srila Prabhupada). The following is a brief account of his life and teachings.

Srila Prabhupada was born on September 1, 1896, the day after Janmashtami (the appearance day of Lord Krishna) in Kolkata. At the time of his birth an astrologer predicted that at the age of seventy, he would leave India to establish 108 temples of Krishna all over the world. Srila Prabhupada certainly displayed great devotion to Lord Sri Krishna from a very early age. His father had given him small Deities of Radha and Krishna which he worshipped daily and at the age of six he organised a blissful Ratha-yatra Krishna festival in his local community which lasted for eight days.

After leaving the prestigious Scottish Churches College, where he studied for his degree, Srila Prabhupada met the person who was to become his spiritual master, Srila Bhaktisiddhanta Sarasvati, who, on their very first meeting, requested Srila Prabhupada to preach Krishna consciousness in the West. It was this instruction that Srila Prabhupada took to heart and dedicated his life to fulfilling.

As a married man, Srila Prabhupada ran a business and spent as much time and money as he could, assisting the preaching mission of his spiritual master. He started a magazine called *'Back to Godhead'* which he wrote, edited, printed and sold single-handedly. He also started a mission in Jhansi called 'The League of Devotees'. Recognizing Srila Prabhupada's philosophical learning and devotion, the society of devotees and scholars in Vrindavana honoured him in 1947 with the title "Bhaktivedanta." In 1959, he was awarded *sannyasa* (the renounced order of life) and after retiring from family life he went to live in the holy village of Vrindavana where he spent his whole time studying and writing, living very simply in one room. Here he worked on his life's masterpiece: a multivolume annotated translation of the eighteen-thousand-verse *Srimad-Bhagavatam* (*Bhagavata Purana*).

Srila Prabhupada figured that since everyone was following the Americans, if he could convince them of Krishna consciousness, then the whole world would eventually follow too. Through a contact he had, Srila Prabhupada managed to get free passage on a regular cargo carrier that was headed for New York. So on August 13, 1965, just a few days before his sixty-ninth birthday when most people would have retired, A.C. Bhaktivedanta Swami Prabhupada set sail to start his preaching mission in the West.

The crossing proved very difficult for Srila Prabhupada, and he suffered two heart attacks. On board the ship there was neither a doctor, nor any medicine that could help him, and he feared a third attack would kill him. That night he had a wonderful dream. Lord Krishna was rowing a boat and reassuring Srila Prabhupada that He would protect him from all danger. Thirty seven days later, Srila Prabhupada arrived in New York knowing no-one, with just 40 rupees in his pocket, a metal suitcase full of his books, an umbrella and a supply of dry cereal, in case he could not find anything vegetarian to eat. But what could one man, who had no visible help or support, was in poor health and who was preaching a message completely unheard of in America, possibly achieve?

In short, between the years 1965 and 1977, His Divine Grace A.C. Bhaktivedanta Swami, or Srila Prabhupada, as his followers affectionately came to know him, had spread the teachings of Lord Krishna to every major city in the world and had formed an international society comprising of thousands of dedicated members. As predicted by his childhood astrologer, he had established 108 Krishna temples, including a thirteen storied building in the heart of the world's most important city, New York, along with magnificent estates spread across six continents. He had circled the globe fourteen times to personally guide the membership of his growing mission. His simple dedication to the order of his spiritual master, and his deep faith and devotion to Krishna had made the words 'Hare Krishna' a household name all over the world, just as Lord Chaitanya had predicted five hundred years ago.

As if this were not enough accomplishment for a person of such advanced age, Srila Prabhupada had also written and published over seventy volumes of books, which have been translated to over twenty-eight languages, tens of millions of which have been distributed throughout the world. He had delivered thousands of lectures, written thousands of letters, and taken part in thousands of conversations with followers, admirers, and critics alike. And he had won the esteem of dozens of important scholars, professors, social figures and politicians, who had genuine appreciation for Srila Prabhupada's contributions to religion, philosophy, and culture. He gained recognition amongst academicians, scholars, religious leaders, political and social figures as possibly the greatest ever exponent of the teachings of Lord Krishna.

"Here for the first time since the days of the Roman Empire is a new Asian religion – that is to say, an Asian religion new to the Western world – being practised by people of Western race. It arose out of nothing in less than twenty years and has become known all over the West...and an important fact in the history of the Western world." — **A.L Basham,** a leading authority on Indian history and religion.

"Besides being a man of deep moral strength, humility, and holiness, he was genuinely renounced. Srila Prabhupada's life. . . is the epitome of his ideal, an ideal

that he set forth for others to follow." — **Dr. J. Stillson Judah,** Professor Emeritus, Graduate Theological Union, Berkeley, California.

"His books are significant contributions to the salvation of mankind." — **Sri Lal Bahadur Shastri,** Former Prime Minister of India.

Srila Prabhupada also instructed that his temples should distribute free *prasadam* (sanctified food) to the poor. This programme is known worldwide as "Food for Life," and **ISKCON, Bangalore,** currently feeds **tens of thousands of poor school children every day** with nourishing foodstuffs under the Akshaya Patra programme All this inspired by the love and deep compassion of a truly saintly person, Srila Prabhupada.

* * *

Model Questions

I. **Answer the following questions by picking the best choice from the options given below:**

1. The name Krishna means
   A) good   B) auspicious   C) all-attractive D) nothing

2. Devaki was married to
   A) Ugrasena   B) Nanda Maharaj
   C) Kamsa   D) Vasudeva

3. Kamsa was a king of the
   A) Raghu dynasty   B) Bhoja dynasty
   C) Yadu dynasty   D) Vrishni dynasty

4. "I promise that if we have any sons I shall present all of them to you to do with as you wish." When were these words spoken?
   A) During the creation of Brahma
   B) During the naming ceremony of Durga-devi
   C) During the send-off of Devaki's marriage party
   D) None of the above

5. What is the name of the stone that was bedecked in the helmet of Krishna?
   A) Kaustubha B) Shyamantaka C) Srivatsa D) Vaidurya

6. Krishna and Balarama used to find out the stock of butter & yogurt kept in a secluded place with the help of
   A) match-light B) effulgence from their ornaments
   C) torchlight   D) moonlight

7. A pure devotee of the Lord is known as
   A) Mayavadi   B) Brahmana
   C) Sannyasi   D) Vaishnava

8. Which elephant was brought to the wrestling arena by Kamsa?
   A) Kuvalyapida   B) Gajendra
   C) Airavata   D) Gajanana

9. Which sage cursed Vidyadhara to assume the form of a serpent?
   A) Vishwamitra   B) Angira
   C) Durvasa   D) Vashista

10. Which among these are imprinted on the soles of Lord Krishna's feet?

    A) Conch   B) Discus   C) Trident   D) Club

II. Fill in the blanks using the appropriate word:

11. Krishna entered the mind of Vasudeva and was then transferred to the _____ of Devaki.

    A) mouth   B) eyes   C) heart   D) body

12. It is difficult for friends and family members to always live together. We are just like _____ floating on the waves of the ocean.

    A) weeds   B) boats   C) oil   D) ducks

13. Krishna is situated as _____ in everyone's heart.

    A) soul   B) supersoul   C) knowledge   D) effulgence

14. In their previous birth, the *gopis* were _____.

    A) ghosts   B) *apsaras*   C) Vedic scholars   D) birds

15. _____ was the family priest of Balarama and Krishna.

    A) Agastya   B) Sandipani   C) Garga Muni   D) Sowbarya

16. The conch shell of Lord Krishna is called _____.

    A) Devadatta   B) Paundra   C) Panchajanya   D) Somadatta

17. _____ was taking care of Hastinapura as a caretaker after the death of Pandu.

    A) Dhritharashtra   B) Vidura   C) Shakuni   D) Bhishma

18. The younger brother of Putana and Bakasura was _____.

    A) Mahishasura   B) Aghasura   C) Aristasura   D) Rakshasa

19. The *devatas'* strength comes from _____.

    A) Shiva   B) Vishnu   C) Indra   D) Brahma

20. Balarama was so called because of His _____.

    A) beauty   B) intelligence   C) honesty   D) strength

III. State whether the following statements are TRUE or FALSE:

21. The cowherd women are also known as *gopis*.

22. Nanda Maharaj went to Dvaraka to pay the annual tax to the government of Kamsa.

23. Putana was washed of all her sins since she offered milk to Balarama.

24. Govardhana puja is also known as Annakuta.

25. The Supreme Personality of Godhead, the Absolute Truth, is controlled by and subject to the desires of His pure devotees.

26. Krishna and Balarama learnt 48 arts and sciences at their master's hermitage.

27. Awarding the desires of *guru* after learning from him is known as Guru-dakshina.

28. Balarama is also known as Anantha Sesha Naga—one who holds all the planets on His millions of heads.

29. The pastime of Aghasura happened when Krishna and His friends were 15 years old.

30. By offending a devotee, a person will go back to Godhead.

IV. Picture based questions:

31. What is the name of the serpent?
    A) Kaliya   B) Vasuki   C) Thakshaka   D) Naga

32. What is the name of the child on the serpent's head?
    A) Arjuna   B) Balarama   C) Krishna   D) Prahlada

33. Where was the serpent living previously?

    A) Mountain   **B)** Cave   **C)** Forest   **D)** Island

34. In which river is this incident taking place?

    A) Yamuna   **B)** Ganga

    C) Saraswati   **D)** Brahmaputra

35. The serpent came there in fear of _____.

    A) Reptiles   **B)** Yamaraja

    C) Garuda   **D)** None of the above

36. What is Krishna doing on the serpent's head?

    A) Beating   **B)** Dancing

    C) Playing   **D)** All of the above

37. Which quality of Krishna is reflected by this incident?

    A) Power   **B)** Mercy

    C) Fearlessness   **D)** All of the above

38. What had the serpent done?

    A) Poisoned the river   **B)** Caught all the frogs

    C) Disturbed Garuda's sleep **D)** None of the above

39. What happened to the serpent at last?

    A) Died   **B)** Fled

    C) Became devotee   **D)** None of the above

40. Who saved the serpent from Krishna?

    A) Balarama   **B)** Wives of the serpent

    C) Arjuna   **D)** None of the above

V. Match the following:

No.	Question		Choice
41.	Indra	**A)**	Kamsa
42.	Kalanemi	**B)**	Krishna
43.	Blue black	**C)**	Father of Kamsa
44.	Ugrasena	**D)**	*Devata* in charge of supplying rain

VI. Read this passage and answer the following questions:

Thus ordered by the Supreme Personality of Godhead, Sri Krishna, Akrura visited Hastinapura, said to be the site of what is now New Delhi. The part of New Delhi still known as Indraprastha is accepted by people in general as the old capital of the Pandavas. The name Hastinapura suggests that the Pandavas kept many *hastis*, or elephants; in the capital. Keeping elephants is very expensive; so to keep many elephants meant that the kingdom was extremely wealthy. Hastinapura, as Akrura saw when he reached it, was full of elephants, horses, chariots and other opulences. At that time the kings of Hasfinapura ruled the whole world. Their fame was widely spread throughout the entire kingdom, and their administration was conducted under the good advice of learned *brahmanas*.

45. Which was known as the old capital of Pandavas?

A) Kurukshetra **B)** Indraprastha

C) Hastinapura **D)** Kalahasthi

46. On whose advice did Akrura visit Hastinapura?

A) Vidura **B)** Somadutta

C) Pandu **D)** Krishna

47. Who were responsible for advising the kings in the matter of administration?

A) *Kshatriyas* **B)** *Shudras*

C) *Brahmanas* **D)** *Vaishyas*

48. What did Akrura see when he reached Hastinapura?

A) Elephants **B)** Horses

C) Chariots **D)** All of the above

49. The name Hastinapura suggests that there were a lot of _____ in the city.

A) elephants **B)** donkeys

C) monkeys **D)** dogs

VII. 50. Write the complete Hare Krishna *maha-mantra* in the space provided in your answer sheet.

Model Answer Sheet

Please shade (⬭) the correct answer.

	A	B	C	D
1.	○	○	○	○
2.	○	○	○	○
3.	○	○	○	○
4.	○	○	○	○
5.	○	○	○	○
6.	○	○	○	○
7.	○	○	○	○
8.	○	○	○	○
9.	○	○	○	○
10.	○	○	○	○

	A	B	C	D
11.	○	○	○	○
12.	○	○	○	○
13.	○	○	○	○
14.	○	○	○	○
15.	○	○	○	○
16.	○	○	○	○
17.	○	○	○	○
18.	○	○	○	○
19.	○	○	○	○
20.	○	○	○	○

	True	False
21.	○	○
22.	○	○
23.	○	○
24.	○	○
25.	○	○
26.	○	○
27.	○	○
28.	○	○
29.	○	○
30.	○	○

	A	B	C	D
31.	○	○	○	○
32.	○	○	○	○
33.	○	○	○	○
34.	○	○	○	○
35.	○	○	○	○
36.	○	○	○	○
37.	○	○	○	○
38.	○	○	○	○
39.	○	○	○	○
40.	○	○	○	○

	A	B	C	D
41.	○	○	○	○
42.	○	○	○	○
43.	○	○	○	○
44.	○	○	○	○

	A	B	C	D
45.	○	○	○	○
46.	○	○	○	○
47.	○	○	○	○
48.	○	○	○	○
49.	○	○	○	○

50. Write the Hare Krishna *mantra* here

_____

_____

Answers for the Model Questions

1. C	11. C	21. True	31. A	41. D
2. D	12. A	22. False	32. C	42. A
3. B	13. B	23. False	33. D	43. B
4. C	14. C	24. True	34. A	44. C
5. D	15. C	25. True	35. C	45. B
6. B	16. C	26. False	36. B	46. D
7. D	17. A	27. True	37. D	47. C
8. A	18. B	28. True	38. A	48. D
9. B	19. B	29. False	39. D	49. A
10. C	20. D	30. False	40. B	

Glossary

Absolute Truth – God, who is independent of everything.

acharya – a spiritual master who teaches by his own personal behaviour.

all-pervading – that which extends throughout.

asura – a demon or nondevotee.

austerities – voluntary acceptance of bodily inconvenience for the sake of spiritual advancement.

avatara – an incarnation of Godhead who descends from the spiritual world.

benediction – a blessing.

Bhagavad-gita – the book that records the spiritual instructions given by Krishna to His friend Arjuna on the battlefield of Kurukshetra.

bhakta – a devotee.

Brahma – the first created living being in the universe.

brahmachari – a celibate student under the guidance of a spiritual master.

Brahman – the impersonal feature of the Absolute Truth.

brahmanas – the spiritual order of society whose occupation is the cultivation of Vedic knowledge.

Brahma-samhita – a scripture written by Lord Brahma in which his authoritative prayers to the Lord are recorded.

cause of all causes – the original cause from which universal creation comes about, as a series of causes and effects. That original cause is Lord Krishna and He is described as *sarva karana karanam*.

Chaitanya Mahaprabhu – the incarnation of Krishna as His own devotee who comes in this age to teach the process of devotional service by chanting the holy names of God.

conditioned soul – a spirit soul who is subjected to the conditions of the material world and has forgotten his real spiritual identity.

conjugal love – the love between husband and wife.

consorts – husbands or wives.

cosmic manifestation – display of the material universes.

demigods -- also known as devas or devatas, they are devotees of Lord Vishnu and are empowered by Him to oversee the various affairs of the material world.

effulgence – rays of brightness.

Ekadashi – a day of fasting which occurs twice a month and which is meant for increasing Krishna consciousness.

expansion – a complete form of the Supreme Lord, Sri Krishna, having all the powers that the Lord possesses.

Gandharvas – celestial denizens of the heavenly planets who sing very beautifully.

Garuda – the giant bird-carrier of Vishnu.

gopis – cowherd girls, specifically the transcendental girl-friends of Lord Krishna.

grihastha – one who is in the householder order of life.

guru – a spiritual master.

illusory energy – the Lord's energy called Maya that puts one in an illusion of one's real identity.

initiated – Formally introduced to spiritual discipline under the guidance of the spiritual master (guru).

internal potency – the Supreme Lord has multiple potencies which are classified into three broad categories – external, internal and marginal. The material world is a manifestation of His external potency, the spiritual world is a manifestation of His internal potency and the living entities (*jiva atmas*) constitute His marginal potency.

jaya – victory.

jnani – someone who engages in mental speculation in pursuit of knowledge.

kadamba – a tree which bears a round yellow flower and which is generally seen only in the Vrindavana area.

karma – fruitive activities or their reactions.

karmi – a fruitive worker.

Kaustubha – a transcendental jewel worn around the neck of the Supreme Personality of Godhead.

kshatriyas – the spiritual order of society whose occupation is governmental administration and military protection of the citizens.

lila – pastimes.

Lord Sesha – Ananta Sesha, the thousand-headed serpent form of the Lord, who sustains the planets on His hoods.

manifested – displayed, exhibited.

material energy – see internal potency.

material opulences – material wealth or riches.

Maya (Mahamaya) – the external, material energy of the Supreme Lord, which covers the conditioned soul and does not allow him to understand the Supreme Personality of Godhead.

Mayavadi – one who adheres to impersonalist or voidist philosophy and does not accept the eternal existence of the transcendental form of the Lord.

miscreants – villains, sinners or criminals.

mukti – liberation.

Mukunda – Lord Krishna, who awards liberation and whose smiling face is like a *kunda* flower.

mystic potencies – superhuman or spiritual powers.

obeisances – bowing down in respect.

Pandavas – the five sons of King Pandu (Yudhishthira, Arjuna, Bhima, Nakula and Sahadeva).

Paramatma – the expansion of the Supreme Lord who lives in the heart of all living entities.

parijata – a type of flower found on the heavenly planets.

parts and parcels – portions, particles.

pastimes – the completely spiritual activities of the Lord, with his devotees.

pious – (*punya karma*) those activities recommended by the Vedas, which will bring about material prosperity in the form of wealth, beauty, intelligence, good birth, fame, etc.

prasadam – food first offered to the Supreme Lord and then distributed.

puffed up – proud.

pure devotees – devotees of the Lord who serve Him without any material desire, simply for His pleasure.

rasa – a transcendental relationship between the individual soul and the Supreme Lord.

rasa-lila – Lord Krishna's transcendental pastime of dancing with the *gopis*.

sannyasi – one who is in the renounced order.

shastras – revealed scriptures.

self realization – to know the real self beyond the designations of body, as a spirit soul (*jiva atma*), in theory and practice.

shudras – the spiritual order of society who are not very intelligent and are unqualified for any work other than menial service.

Shyamasundara – a name of Krishna. *Shyama* means 'blackish' and *sundara* means 'very beautiful.'

Srimad-Bhagavatam – the authoritative Vedic scripture that deals exclusively with the pastimes of the Personality of Godhead and His devotees.

Sudarshana – the wheel that is the personal weapon of Vishnu or Krishna.

tapasya – austerity.

tilaka – a clay mark that decorates the faces of Krishna and His devotees.

transcendental – spiritual, beyond this material world.

Tulasi – a great devotee in the form of a plant, who is very dear to Lord Krishna.

Vaishnava – a devotee of the Supreme Lord Vishnu or Krishna.

vaishyas – the agricultural community in Vedic culture, who protect cows and cultivate crops.

Vishnu – the Supreme Lord; an expansion of Lord Krishna for the creation and maintenance of the material world.

whorl – circular arrangement of leaves or flowers.

yajna – sacrifice.

yoga – the process of linking with the Supreme.

Yogamaya – the principal internal (spiritual) potency of the Supreme Lord.

yogi – one who practices *yoga*.

Books by
   His Divine Grace A. C. Bhaktivedanta Swami Prabhupada:

Bhagavad-gita As It Is
Srimad-Bhagavatam (18 vols.; with disciples)
Sri Chaitanya-charitamrta (9 vols.)
Teachings of Lord Chaitanya
The Nectar of Devotion
The Nectar of Instruction
Sri Isopanisad
Easy Journey to Other Planets
Krishna Consciousness: The Topmost Yoga System
Krishna, The Supreme Personality of Godhead
Perfect Questions, Perfect Answers
Teachings of Lord Kapila, the Son of Devahuti
Transcendental Teachings of Prahlada Maharaja
Dialectic Spiritualism-A Vedic View of Western Philosophy
Teachings of Queen Kunti
Krishna, the Reservoir of Pleasure
The Science of Self-Realization
The Path of Perfection
Search for Liberation
Life Comes from Life
The Perfection of Yoga
Beyond Birth and Death
On the Way to Krishna
Raja-vidya: The King of Knowledge
Elevation to Krishna Consciousness
Krishna Consciousness: The Matchless Gift
The Narada-bhakti-sutra (with disciples)
The Mukunda-mala-stotra (with disciples)
A Second Chance
The Journey of Self-Discovery
The Laws of Nature
The Sword of Knowledge
Back to Godhead magazine (founder)